T0043905

Reworked

Reworked

Putting Health and Happiness
at the Centre of Your Career

Dr Stephanie Fitzgerald

NICHOLAS BREALEY
PUBLISHING

London • Boston

First published in Great Britain by Nicholas Brealey Publishing in 2023
An imprint of John Murray Press
A division of Hodder & Stoughton Ltd,
An Hachette UK company

1

A CIP catalogue record for this title is available from the British Library

Trade Paperback ISBN 978 1 399 80669 5
eBook ISBN 978 1 399 80671 8

Typeset by KnowledgeWorks Global Ltd.

Printed and bound in Great Britain by Clays Ltd, Elcograf S.p.A.

John Murray Press policy is to use papers that are natural, renewable and recyclable
products and made from wood grown in sustainable forests. The logging and
manufacturing processes are expected to conform to the environmental regulations of the
country of origin.

John Murray Press
Carmelite House
50 Victoria Embankment
London EC4Y 0DZ

www.nicholasbrealey.com

To everyone who has ever had a bad day at work. I've got you.

Contents

Introduction

Seventy-nine per cent of us are in the wrong job. If you have been feeling anywhere from mildly dissatisfied (60 per cent of us) through to deeply unhappy at work (19 per cent), or have had periods throughout your career where you have felt lost or have struggled, you are not alone. A Gallup survey of the global workforce[1] found that only 21 per cent of us feel engaged in our work. Let that sink in. You and four of your friends are having dinner together and only one of you around the table is in the right job.

Simple probability means that 79 per cent of us cannot just be unlucky. We cannot have fallen into the wrong job and become disengaged by chance. It suggests that we are set up to fail. It tells us that we are somehow doing work wrong. It suggests that the very framework of how we approach our work is broken. The whole system needs to be reworked.

We've never learned how to work well

While almost all of us will have to work, no one has ever taught us *how* to work. No one ever sat down with us and told us how to be happy and healthy in the workplace. How to get our needs met. How to support ourselves, and others, as we navigate the complexities of work. Doesn't it seem odd to you that something that is so unavoidably fundamental to our human experience is never truly explored?

We're not taught how to work in school. We're taught to pass exams to get a good job, but there is no discussion as to what a 'good' job means. We don't examine what a good job may look like for us as an individual. We grow up with vague ideas and notions around salary, status and possible career pathways, with no real understanding of where we fit into that picture.

I'm a clinical psychologist by background and a neuropsychologist by specialism. I've worked in mental health for two decades, and I left the UK's National Health Service (NHS) to work as a health and wellbeing consultant in 2013. Working in this area hasn't been easy. Health and safety advisors are everywhere, and so you could be forgiven for thinking that I had a ready-made tribe of people willing to support my mission to make the workplace a healthier space. However, the reality is that when it comes to health and safety, the health is whispered and the SAFETY is shouted.

I realized that no one really cares if employees are healthy or not: as long as the company is meeting basic safety regulations, it is considered a job well done. I decided this wasn't good enough. The typical health and safety metrics needed expanding to support the evolving workplace. I developed metrics that ensured people were able to be, and work, well.

You'll often see the acronym HSE in the workplace. If discussing the function, then that's 'health, safety and environment'. If describing a job title, then that's 'health and safety executive'. I wanted an acronym that put employees at the centre of the workplace, and so I adapted these well-known short hands to create my own: HHSE. Happy. Healthy. Safe. Engaged. My tagline for workplace wellbeing, and my career, was born. Happy, healthy, safe and engaged are the true markers of working well. These are the fundamentals of our working lives, and should be a constant in our careers.

Why happy, healthy, safe and engaged?

Being happy, healthy, safe and engaged is an integrative approach. It brings you, your health and your happiness into the centre of your work, regardless of your role. You are no longer battling your work, exhausted from a juggling act. It's an approach that gives you energy, rather than depletes it. Yes, you'll have challenging days, but within a context that energizes, encourages and invigorates you. Instead of expending your energy at work, you will be recharging it. This is regardless of, maybe even in spite of, the job you do.

Work has become an all-consuming identifier. We're not achieving work–life balance, a concept we strive for, but ultimately fail at. We cannot carve our hours up into a neat pie chart, where one aspect of living does not cross over or impact another. Yet we pit our work and our life against each other. Work is something we do; life is something we crave. It's just not working well.

We push ourselves to progress, then need to recover from burnout. We take annual leave to escape. We collapse on the sofa and abandon passion projects in favour of numbing ourselves with our addiction of choice, be it alcohol, food or TV boxsets, simply to block out the working day. We squeeze more and more into our own time and put increasing pressure on ourselves to improve our wellbeing. We never consider that the one place we attend every day could be the same place to fuel us. The place we spend a third of our life. Our workplace. We don't have to pit work against life; instead work can support all aspects of our lives. We just need to know how.

HHSE is the fuel for your engine. It is proactive and not reactive. You wouldn't complete a long car journey and wait until the end to fill your car with fuel. Instead, you recognize that you need the fuel in order to complete your journey. The same is true of your career. You cannot work flat out for years and then shift your attention to your wellbeing. Being happy, healthy, safe and engaged is not something you need to wait until retirement to achieve. By reworking how we work, we can ensure our HHSE is supported and promoted throughout our career.

People often talk about happier employees in terms of the positive impact on a business, citing that happier employees are more productive employees and that increased wellbeing creates a huge boost for business. There is no denying this, and the research supports this time and again. However, this book isn't about work, it is about *you*. When you are happy, healthy, safe and engaged, you can give work the right amount of energy and time and not feel a clash with your home life. A seamless flow of supportive energy will exist between work and home. There will be no 'repair' needed because work won't harm you in the first place. You can take holidays for a love of travel, not a need to escape. Leveraging the skills of HHSE allows you to make work *work* for you. Work will be your charging pad, supporting and boosting every element of your wellbeing.

HHSE means you can sit alongside yourself as an ally, rather than battle the 'work you' who is tired. Even if you are in a job that you are completely dispassionate about, you'll see positive benefits of reworking it to be more HHSE. The tools learned will empower you to make good decisions for your future, have skills to support yourself through every career, and build your confidence. You don't need the perfect job to be happy. You need the four pillars of happy, healthy, safe and engaged.

As Annie Dillard says in her book *The Writing Life*, 'How we spend our days is, of course, how we spend our lives.'[2] Doesn't it make sense to spend them happy, healthy, safe and engaged?

This isn't a book about positive thinking or making the best of a bad situation. As a consultant, I work with companies to ensure employees meet the four foundational underpinnings of good work. If they don't, then I use neuroscience, psychology and evidence-based best practice to get them to that place. These are the tools I will be sharing in this book. You will learn how to have your best day at work ever, regardless of the job you are in, or the salary you earn. I am going to teach you to bring your wellness into the centre of your career. Prepare to work, well.

'This is Steph. She does the hand-holding'

Welcome to my early career in workplace wellbeing. The above quotation was how I was introduced to the board of directors within an NHS Trust, part of the UK's healthcare system. I had just successfully completed a pilot study which hypothesized that, if you took better care of doctors and nurses, then patients would be discharged from hospital more quickly, be healthier and be less likely to need readmission (spoiler alert: it works). This was a turning point in my career.

What had begun as a side project, alongside my full-time clinical psychologist role, had me gripped. Having always worked on a one-to-one basis in therapy, or through delivering interventions to very small groups, here I had witnessed the incredibly positive impact that some straightforward workplace wellbeing initiatives had on hundreds of people. Not only that, but I saw sustained, continuous improvement, which was still present at a six-month follow-up. I became almost evangelical about the amazing impact being happier and healthier at work could have, both on individuals and those around them. As I replicated these results again and again, across different teams and different Trusts, I couldn't understand why everyone wasn't talking about this. I became determined to share the information so that everyone could benefit. As I have already stated, most of us, out of financial necessity, have to work. Doesn't it make sense for us to also work *well*?

As you can see from the rather derogatory introduction I was given, not everyone was quite so enthusiastic. In fact, at that point in time, staff wellbeing was not valued very highly at all. When I first started talking to people, health and wellbeing was openly mocked in the workplace, even in a healthcare setting, often being referred to as the 'pink and fluffy stuff'. I was told that 'people aren't at work to have fun', and I experienced cuts to, if not total withdrawal of, my budget as soon as companies had 'ticked the box' and then promptly lost interest. Those times proved crucial in developing what truly works. When the money stopped, I had to get creative and found that I could positively impact individuals, companies and entire industries using no-cost or low-cost techniques. Now, I want to share these with you.

Working in this field has felt as though I watched an amazing boxset ten years ago and only in the last few years have others caught up and started chatting animatedly about it. I'm so delighted to see the conversation grow, and now it is rare that a company doesn't consider its employees' wellbeing to some degree, whether that's solely through a production and profit lens, or because they truly care and feel a moral obligation to support their staff.

Although it has been amazing to see the conversation increase, in among the volume is a lot of unhelpful noise.

Wellbeing at work for so long has been confused with lettuce in the canteen and yoga on the lawn, neither of which constitutes a wellbeing strategy. Of course, there are huge benefits to healthy eating and exercise at work, but all the subsidized salad in the world cannot force an individual who isn't engaged in their job to become happier in the workplace. Also, when it comes to wellbeing, one size most definitely does not fit all. It's all very well offering yoga, but if your shop floor set-up means that people are penalized for stopping production, then when are they expected to attend? It is our approach to workplace wellness that needs to be more flexible, not employees.

The unspoken privilege of wellbeing

The shift following the global coronavirus pandemic has, at last, put the employment market in the hands of employees. Companies are having to compete to attract and retain talent, and employees are looking industries in the eye and saying: 'Paying my salary is no longer enough – what else can you offer me?' This is leading to more conversations than ever about employee wellbeing, but is also highlighting an unspoken privilege in the workplace. For too long, wellness at work has been the reserve of those fortunate enough to have roles where they have flexibility, control and autonomy.

However, the conversation gets very quiet when we start to talk about the shop floor, the frontline workers, those on trade union-mandated shift patterns. What about those who don't work a 9–5 and don't have an office laptop or phone? What message are we sending about work? Are we satisfied that it's possible to be happy and healthy in work as long as you can work from home?

I attended a conference recently which highlighted why companies cannot create one-size solutions and expect success in improving wellbeing for all employees. A head of human resources presented an initiative she had been running in her company, where the company encouraged its senior leaders to share experiences of collecting their children from school. The idea was to highlight the emphasis on wellbeing and making the working day flexible, and it was met with a lot of admiration.

At the time I was working for a manufacturing company, and I thought of all the people I worked with who would love to spend more time with their kids, but who had no option to break their shift pattern to do so. How much they would have enjoyed taking an hour out of their working day to do the school pick-up and share more of the moments that they typically miss out on. No one was talking about their wellbeing. No one was addressing how we can support them in the workplace. The rising inequality in our workplaces is becoming clearer and it needs addressing. This presentation was a great example of positive intent but a lack of inclusivity. There is privilege in wellbeing, and only by taking control of our own wellbeing can we overcome the divide.

Surely my wellbeing at work is my company's responsibility?

I have had the privilege to work across many different industries and organizations ranging from the finance sector, through to Premier League football clubs, through to the atomic weapons business, and throughout them all, I've noticed patterns. Companies across the board are showing an increased interest in the health and wellbeing of their employees. It is an issue that is becoming harder to ignore, as employees themselves are coming to the table with an interest in their wellbeing at work, and asking questions when that appears compromised. I rarely meet a company director these days who doesn't have some sort of objective around workforce wellbeing.

However, while both employers and employees want positive and healthy experiences, no one really seems to know what to do. Because companies don't know what approach to take, they throw money around and hope it's doing something. When no tangible difference is felt, companies shrug and say to their employees, 'Well, I did my bit, over to you.' The simple truth is: *you* are the biggest expert in your own wellness. You will spend your lifetime learning what sets you alight, what sparks joy, what gets you out of bed with a spring in your step. The experience of wellness is too personal and subjective to be handed over to an external entity that has never walked a step in your shoes.

We look to work to solve issues that are within our gift to resolve and which work simply cannot. Not every role can adapt to provide a solution, and so we need to take more control. We have to do the work on our own wellbeing, and if we do, then we will gain time, energy, focus, drive, ambition and, much more importantly, the health, happiness, safety and engagement that we deserve, yet are missing out on.

Wellbeing approaches need to be personalized, and they need to be accommodating. Sometimes what we need from different people at different times can change on a daily basis. We cannot expect a company to be able to cover every aspect of our wellbeing and support us to an adequate degree. We need to utilize our own expertise in our own wellness. It needs to be a joint endeavour between you and your work.

While your company may have some stake in your wellbeing, the buck stops with you. If work isn't making you happy, then you need the tools to be happy in work. This is why it is so essential that we don't leave workplace wellbeing in the hands of organizations. We need to have a greater understanding of how to work and how to engage in our roles, in a way that puts our HHSE needs first. Don't wait for work to improve your wellbeing. Use the techniques outlined in this book and enjoy the improvements to your wellbeing in work.

But if I'm unhappy at work, shouldn't I just quit?

Maybe. But know this: quitting is a reaction, not a solution. There are good reasons why I don't advocate simply quitting even when work sucks. Quitting won't solve anything if we don't first make the fundamental changes needed to become happy, healthy, safe and engaged at work. As we will explore, quitting can actually exacerbate and strengthen unhealthy work patterns, and we need to do the work *before* we leave our role. Much like leaving one terrible relationship in the hope that the next one will save us, quitting a job where we are unhappy won't automatically mean we will be any happier in the next one. There is work to be done before we quit.

This book is not designed to teach you to see rainbows where there are only storm clouds. I absolutely appreciate that sometimes within a role there are seemingly no redeeming features and you want to leave. However, believe me when I say you can't quit while there is still so much work to be done. The work needed to ensure that you have your best day at work, every day. It is possible for you to feel happy and healthy in the workplace, although it may have been some time since you felt either. That isn't your fault. No one has ever taught you how to be at the centre of your work, your career, how to get the most out of your role, and how to truly be happy, healthy, safe and engaged in the workplace. Until now.

So no, I'm not going to encourage you to pack it all in and jump ship. Nor am I going to suggest you should turn your side-hustle into a hugely successful business alongside your already demanding (yet likely disengaging) job. Frankly, I am sick to death of the 'love it or leave it' oversimplified insta-wisdom about workplace wellness. If you have bills to pay, and food to put on the table, then you simply do not have the luxury of giving up work and following your dream. You may not even have the luxury of dreaming, and such advice is irritating and patronizing at best. Having to work means you need the fundamentals to support your wellbeing in the workplace. Once you have that established, then you can make great decisions about your future.

Happy, healthy, safe and engaged is more than a strapline for me, it is a passion. I live and breathe it. I firmly believe that we can and we should be happy and healthy at work, and that this is possible in any role. Working full-time means we will clock up an average 81,396 hours at work in our lifetime.[3] Let's spend them well.

1

Rethinking Work

Pretty much everything we've ever been told, or sold, about work is wrong. This sounds extreme, but there are so many myths around work which continually confuse and challenge us and, crucially, lead us to feel that we are doing it wrong. After all, why don't we have our dream job yet? Why aren't we being promoted? Why aren't we CEO already? If we are all these things, then why aren't we happy?

The notions of work, what work can do for us, and how we approach work are confusing and continually fuelled by false claims, memes and myths. Much of what we are told is refracted through someone else's experience, beliefs and perceptions, which makes the advice impossible to replicate, because it is not related to our own situation. One individual's idea of a perfect job is not going to be perfect for all.

Myth-busting in this space is important because the more false information we have about work, the more we believe we are doing it wrong and then blame ourselves for things going awry. When we accept the myths, we judge ourselves by impossible standards and markers, none of which has a place in the modern workplace. The myths that we are told can block our path to being HHSE at work, and we need to unpick these beliefs so they stop getting in our way. So, let's bust a few myths and alleviate some pressure and guilt so we have the headspace and energy to focus on what actually matters: working, well.

Myth 1: If you do what you love, you'll never work a day in your life – Marc Anthony

This is the biggest myth that exists in the modern workplace, yet it is an idea that we insist on repeating, sharing and advocating as true workplace wellness. This simply Is. Not. True. You WILL work, even if you absolutely adore your job. In fact, you are likely to work harder and put in more hours if you love the work that you do.[1] The notion that, somehow, we will never feel as though we are working hard if we do something we love is preposterous.

Meet Casey

Oh my word, yes I love my job. I always wanted to be a professional potter, but it is exhausting! I create in the morning from 5 a.m. onwards, but I definitely don't leap out of bed. I set an alarm, swear and grumble as I stick the kettle on bleary-eyed and question what I am doing roughly once every minute of that first hour. Then there is all the work that comes around the creativity. Maintaining websites, marketing, promoting. Even the creativity. Although mostly I love it, I have to constantly battle inner criticism and resist the temptation to smash my work at the end of the day. I feel doubt and worry that it is not good enough. Every day is hard work, but I do believe that the work is worth it. I like the process and the outcome enough to want to persevere. I do look at other jobs sometimes and think 'that would be easier/less stressful' but it wouldn't be this, and I absolutely believe this is what I would rather be doing with my time. So yes, I love my job but I definitely do the damn work!

The notion of 'never working a day' speaks to the idea that we accept that work has to feel like drudgery unless we find our perfect job, where somehow we will be in such a state of bliss that we won't even notice the work.

A more realistic view of work means a more attainable view of work and therefore one that is more encouraging and motivating. Let's accept that work will be work. We will have pockets of work that we love, and pockets of work that we don't. What we want to focus on is how happy, healthy, safe and engaged each of these pockets makes us feel. This is where we should put our focus and energy, not in some unrealistic notion of a workplace nirvana. If you find that you are still very much working day to day and have never had the experience of feeling as though going to work is a holiday, then that's OK. It feels like work because it *is* work.

Myth 2: Everyone else knows what they want to be when they grow up

Working with 16–18-year-olds, I found that one of their biggest stresses was not knowing what they wanted to do next. They would often cite friends and peers who knew exactly what they wanted to do next, which course they were going to study, and what steps were next for them, and they felt they were failing by not knowing what direction they themselves wanted to take.

Our brains hate uncertainty and crave knowing what is next and what the plan is, which makes the decision points in life really stressful and anxiety-provoking. Sometimes our brains are more comfortable with a rubbish plan than with having no plan at all.

We leave academic environments with very little experience of autonomy and are suddenly given free rein. Go where you want to go, do what you want to do, be who you want to be. These are challenging concepts for individuals who have never had the freedom to explore these ideas, and may even have spent their academic career having their individuality squashed and oppressed. No wonder we can be confused from a young age. Ironically, once we make the decision about our future, the doubt and uncertainty don't stop there.

When I worked in a university, the biggest cause of anxiety I saw in students was fear that they had made the wrong choice. This was particularly evident once tuition fees were increased and the average UK student (paying the highest tuition fees in the world[2]) became mindful that they were accruing in the region of £45,000 of student debt. The fear that they were studying the wrong course or moving into the wrong career, and gaining a large debt to show for it, was crippling. No wonder they were anxious. Only 21 per cent of college graduates use most or all of their education in their work/career.[3]

Even if we make a choice we like, the average worker will change jobs 12 times across their lifetime.[4] If we assume a rough average of 50 years spent in the workplace, then this equates to changing jobs roughly every four years. Ninety-one per cent of millennials expect to change jobs every three years, and the average employee will change their career entirely at least five times.[5]

So, no. Not everyone knows what they want to be or do when they grow up. Even if they do, this will change as they move through their career. As I type this, 70 per cent of the global workforce is actively looking for a change in career. How liberating to realize that we are supposed to doubt and can use that as curiosity to explore, progress, move, discover and uncover who we can be, at different points, in different jobs. We aren't meant to be career monogamists, and if you don't know what your one career is supposed to be, then that's because you have several careers to explore ahead of you.

Myth 3: My work defines me

This weird belief is reinforced socially when, on being introduced to new people, inevitably the question 'What do you do?' will be asked, and people never mean 'for fun'.

This is a real indictment of society. We ask people how they spend their working day, almost as though there is an assumption that they don't do anything else. The fun, interesting and exciting parts of someone almost always lie in what they do outside work, what they choose to do, what their hobbies are. OK, so you're a lawyer, but who are you actually?

Believing work defines us makes everything about our career a little bit more challenging. When we invest too much of our identity in our work, we are left vulnerable if that situation changes, especially if unexpectedly, through redundancy or business closure for example. Also, it can lead to biased and assumptive conclusions about us as a person. When people hear I am a psychologist, they make many assumptions about my personality, my relationship, my family and so on. Some of these assumptions can be amusing, some can be infuriating, almost none is true.

It is important to see that work is something we do, not who we are. A profession is not a personality.[6]

Myth 4: I'm not good at certain jobs

We get very fixed ideas about what we can and can't do for work, a habit which is instilled from our earliest years in education onwards. In school we are assessed, measured and reviewed, and then the feedback we receive tells us whether we are 'good' at certain subjects.

None of these assessments is designed to do anything more than capture a snapshot of ability at a point in time. They don't take into account our ability to learn, our focus, our ambition or our actual overall ability. This is problematic when, in the UK, we are guided to use this feedback to inform our subject choices between the ages of 12–14 years old,[7] which in turn guides our higher education choices and later our earliest careers. How crazy is that? We are being guided towards what we should embark on for the rest of our lives, based upon which subjects we are 'good at' in our earliest teenage years. Would you let 13-year-old you make any other decisions and expect to live with them for ever? It doesn't make sense.

Many mock the idea of 'a job for life' as an old-fashioned extreme with no place in the modern workforce, but our view of education could be seen as even more antiquated. Why do we assume that something we were good at when we were 11 is going to provide a great source of aptitude when we are 21 or 51 years old?

Being told we are good or not good at a subject in our formative years can be very damaging. I have worked with many adults who don't run their own business, despite wanting to, because they were told they were no good at maths, the upshot being they don't believe they could manage the financial side of running their own business. Individuals who are told they are not creative never pick up a paintbrush or learn the joy of expressing themselves simply because their younger selves believed the adult who told them so. We may assume we are not creative because we weren't good at art, but we might be an excellent problem-solver, a skill which requires high-level creative thinking. We need to stop limiting ourselves based on our experiences at school. They don't apply here.

There are very real barriers to progression and acceptance into certain roles, without us limiting ourselves through misinformed and outdated beliefs. The World Bank cites 104 economies with labour laws that restrict the type of jobs women can undertake, and when and where they are permitted to work. It estimates that this affects the employment choices of 2.7 billion women.[8] However we identify, we need to make sure our own beliefs are not a further limiting barrier, adding to the external complications of the workforce. We can absolutely be 'good' at whatever job we set our minds to, but we have to have faith in ourselves, and we need to understand a little bit more about our brains to overcome this doubt.

Myth 5: I'm not wired to do certain jobs

Following on from myth 4, that we are not good at certain jobs, many adults believe that their brain is wired to work a certain way. We used to hold a belief that our brains were done developing by the time we reached adulthood and so who we were and who we could be were already determined. This isn't true, but has been further fuelled by ideas in popular culture which suggest we are either left-brain or right-brain people. The assumption here is that people who use the right-brain more are more creative, thoughtful and subjective, whereas left-brain people are more logical, detail-oriented and analytical. However, research has repeatedly shown that this simply isn't how our brains work. While there are absolutely some different abilities housed in different areas of the brain, for example languages on the left and attention on the right, there is no evidence of individual differences favouring one hemisphere over another. In other words, people do not have a left or right dominant side.[9]

Having a fixed belief about our abilities is to ignore everything we know about neuroplasticity in the brain. Neuroplasticity is a process of development whereby our neurons adapt and change during our entire lifetime. This amazing process in the brain means that as humans we can develop and progress in anything that we set our minds to. It is the difference between beliefs about talent versus practice. There may be some activities or ways of thinking that our brains already have strong and established neural networks for, and we can think of these as 'talents'. This means that certain tasks and activities will come easily to us, and we can think of ourselves as being 'naturally good' at something, such as languages. However, very simple, consistent exposure means that we can learn almost anything.

Imagine your neural pathways are footpaths through a forest. As you walk through the forest, you have well-worn pathways which are familiar and which your brain uses as short cuts. Our brains are inherently efficient (which is a polite way of saying lazy). They will find the quickest short cut to any conclusion. So, if you try to learn something new, but you have a belief or are told that you are no good at that activity, then your brain will follow the path most trodden and you'll fail. But if you believe that you can change, and you put the hours in, then you can train your brain to take a different path.

Imagine you have always turned left at a fork in the pathways. You are familiar with the left-hand turn, you know the route of the left-hand turn, you don't have to think or worry once you turn left. This is your brain on an established neural pathway. It is quick, it is easy, it happens automatically. Imagine then, one day, you decide to learn something new and turn right. This is challenging, there is no obvious path, your brain isn't sure what is happening, you may have thoughts of failure, getting lost, feeling anxious. Your brain will want you to continue turning left.

If on day one, you turn right, you will have to pick your way through the trees. You'll need to flatten some leaves underfoot, and maybe duck and dive a little, but you will find a route through the trees. If you do the same the next day, it will still be challenging and you will be struggling to create your new pathway. But if you continue to turn right then, day after day, that pathway will become clearer and easier to navigate and before you know it you will have created a new path that is becoming easier to use. This is neuroplasticity. This is your brain carving out a new way of working.

Let's say you never believed you were good at maths. Every time you try to do some maths, your brain turns left down the lazy 'we can't do that' pathway and so you never learn differently. But then one day you decide to try. The first foray into maths is going to be challenging, frustrating and difficult. But the more you do it, the easier it will become. It is perseverance, not talent, that creates new neural pathways. It is perseverance that means we can be whoever and learn whatever skill we want. It may not be the easiest task, but the more we do it, the more we learn and the more we develop.

This is why we need to let go of the extremely self-limiting belief of not being wired for certain jobs. We can train our brain to do anything but we need to put in the time, and that means deciding if it is worth our time.

James Clear, author of *Atomic Habits*,[10] interviewed an Olympic coach and asked, 'What is the difference between elite athletes and the rest of us?' The coach replied: 'The ability to push through boredom.' Of course, there are days when elite athletes don't want to train. Days when they don't want to push themselves, are bored and fed up and want to stay in bed. But they don't. Truthfully, the only thing standing between you and what you want to do, from a brain perspective, is showing up. So don't let your brain, or anyone else, convince you that you cannot do something. You absolutely can.

Myth 6: Working hard means working long hours

The words 'work' and 'hard' appear to be intertwined. We praise people for 'working really hard', but it is important to separate out determination and ambition from unhealthy work practices.

We have some very odd role models in the modern working world. We have hugely revered business gurus preaching to millions across social media platforms about how hard they have worked, equating hard work with long and challenging hours. They encourage this practice and attribute their success to it, by stating that if you work double the hours that someone else does then you will get twice as much done. Well, far be it from me to contradict the gurus but ... they're wrong.

This approach to work is extremely outdated and ignores everything we know about how our brains work. While said gurus dedicated many additional hours above the average working week and admit making many personal sacrifices in the process, one could argue they have been successful in spite of, not because of, their working practices.

Research shows we become less productive the more hours we work. In fact, anything over 55 hours becomes meaningless, with research showing that those who work an additional 15 hours (bringing their working week total to 70 hours) will achieve nothing further. An extra 15 hours at work, for literally no gain. Research also shows that, if you work over 50 hours, you are less effective than if you had worked fewer than 30 hours.

Our perception of long hours is also likely skewed. In the same way we as humans tend to underestimate how much we eat, we tend to overestimate how much we work. Working adults in the USA tend to overestimate their working hours by 5–10 per cent, with some professions including teachers and lawyers overestimating by up to 20 per cent.[11]

One could argue that those gurus claiming a 100–120-hour work week (I'm not calling them liars, but the maths and sustainability of their claims simply do not add up) actually reaped no greater rewards than if they had worked half of that.

Our brains need consistency, rest, processing time and the space to reflect. This allows us to problem-solve and perform at our best. Protecting your brain health is one of the most important ways you can achieve workplace wellness. It's how you stay creative, have new ideas and remain innovative. Believing that hard work and productivity are the result of very long hours is damaging. Wearing your brain out in this way, without adequate rest and recovery, is the easiest way to achieve burnout and little else. Working hard does not mean working long hours.

Myth 7: Money is the marker of success

Richard Branson, founder of the Virgin Group, describes how happiness, not money, is the marker of his success. Branson wrote in an infamous LinkedIn post: 'It's a common misconception that money is every entrepreneur's metric for success. It's not, and nor should it be.'[12]

In writing about money, I know I am dangerously close to sounding as if I'm taking a very irritating line.

If you are struggling to feed your family, or are overwhelmed by bills or debt, being told that money isn't important is infuriating, so please don't misunderstand me. I am not saying that money doesn't matter. It does. But it isn't a marker of success. More money does not mean you have more success; it merely means that you have more money.

The definition of success is so much broader, subjective and more nuanced than money. Success means different things in different lines of work and is dependent on what the purpose of a job is. For a brain surgeon to be successful, they need to operate on patients without damaging their brains or negatively impacting their lives. What they earn is irrelevant. If you are a Formula 1 driver, then success is defined by how many races you win. Success is how successfully you complete your job. Nothing more, nothing less.

The success equals money mentality is a long-held and deeply engrained belief within society; so many of us grew up believing that earning more money was what we should aim for throughout our career. If we then don't earn what we deem to be enough money, we consider ourselves unsuccessful. Chapter 4 further explores the limitations of the money mindset, and considers alternative markers of success and why focusing on money can actually prevent us from earning more.

Questions for reflection

- Do you hold with any of the commonly held myths described above?
- Have any of these held you back?
- In the past have any of these myths got in the way of how happy, healthy, safe and engaged you've felt in your job?
- Is there a different viewpoint you can adopt moving forward to bring you more authentically into the centre of your career?
- What other myths can you let go of today?

Reworking myths

- Work will always feel like work, with pockets of work we love, and other pockets that we don't.
- It doesn't matter if we don't know what we want to do for a career as we will change jobs and even our careers frequently. What matters is being open to and exploring what we want to do now, what works for us and what we want to focus on.

- What we were good at in school does not dictate what we are good at now.
- Our brains are wired for continuous growth, learning and development. We can do anything we put our minds to.
- Working hard does not mean working long hours.
- Money is not a marker of success.

What follows throughout the book are the techniques and ideas that will move you away from the myths. You are going to learn everything that we should be told about work, from day one, in order to best protect our health and wellbeing throughout our careers. It's never too late to learn how to be happy, healthy, safe and engaged at work. Let's start that journey together, now. It's time to start working ... *well*.

2

Start by Stopping

'Start by stopping' is one of my favourite phrases. It's a mantra I apply both in and out of the workplace as a reminder to pause. In an impatient world, it is so tempting to jump in without direction. When we feel overwhelmed or under pressure, we just want to get going. Eyes down, head down, crack on. However, our brains are not designed to work that way. We cannot make good decisions when we are unable to think straight, and if we aren't careful, we can be halfway down a track before we realize this isn't the direction that we wanted to travel in. Whenever things feel challenging, overwhelming or just plain off, start by stopping. It is also the best way to embark on any new process, including this one. So, take a breath. Take a moment. Take a step back. Let's start by stopping.

In the pause you create, ask yourself a very important question.

Are you OK?

Now ask yourself again: are *you* OK? Notice what informs your answer.

When I worked in the NHS, people would come to me and ask, 'Steph, are you OK?' but that wasn't really what they were asking. The question 'Are you OK?' actually meant 'Is your ward OK? Are your patients OK? Is anyone presenting in crisis or at risk? Are your case notes up to date? Is your team OK? Have you liaised with the nurses?' and so on. I would rapidly consider all these elements before replying, 'Yes, I am OK.'

We've lost the art of checking in with ourselves. Working in businesses where we are accountable to others means we consider everything and everyone around us, putting our own needs last – if we bring them into the equation at all. If we are asked, 'Are you OK?', we may consider orders, clients, others' demands, and our perceived or desired progress. If we are managers, we may consider, 'Is my team OK? Is everyone around me OK? Are my bosses happy?' It may be that where we work no one ever asks us if we are OK, and so we have forgotten to ask ourselves.

So often we reply in auto-mode. Someone says, 'How are you?' and we answer, 'Fine, thanks. How are you?' We have probably all taken part in conversations where we are absolutely not OK but for whatever reason we simply answer, 'Fine, thanks', and move the chat along. We can become so used to answering this question automatically and assuming that, if those around us are OK, then *we* must also be OK, that we have forgotten to answer the question truthfully.

So, once again, start by stopping. Pause. Take a breath. Forget everyone else for just a moment and focus on *you*. Are you OK?

Why now?

You will have your own reasons for picking up a book focusing on wellness at work. Was it a bad day? A series of bad days? Was it a desire to make things better? Are you feeling a bit stuck and mildly unfulfilled, or are you desperately unhappy and you'd switch jobs tomorrow if you could?

Understanding your 'Why now?' helps give you the motivation and focus to put in place what is needed to rebalance. It's easy to lose sight of our 'why' in relation to work. We have a vague idea that things will get better, and we automatically assume we are OK because we don't check in with ourselves, as already noted. It is sometimes only when we get too tired and too fed up that we realize how bad things have become or that we are deeply unhappy and need to make a change. Start thinking about why now, and not some distant point in the future, is the perfect time to start your journey to working well.

When did you last have a good day at work?

Consider your last two weeks at work and answer the ten questions below, responding either 'yes' or 'no'. If you're not currently working, then mentally place yourself back into a typical two-week period in your last role and consider the questions below within that context.

Activity: You and work

Don't think about your answers for too long – go with your gut. Yes or no.

1 Have you felt energized and excited by your job? Y/N

2 Have you managed a great work–life balance? Y/N

3 Have you had positive conversations about work? Y/N

4 Have you been complimented on your work? Y/N

5 Would you recommend your exact job (e.g. the work you actually do day-to-day) to someone else? Y/N

6 Have you found it easy to feel motivated and get up and get going every day? Y/N

7 Have you felt a strong connection with your colleagues, team and/or clients? Y/N

8 Have you made healthy choices after work (e.g. eating healthy meals, exercising, avoiding alcohol, prioritizing sleep)? Y/N

9 Have you felt fulfilled and satisfied every day? Y/N

10 Have you thought 'I cannot wait to get to work tomorrow'? Y/N

Take a moment to reflect on your answers. If you answered mostly 'yes', then congratulations! It sounds as though you have had a great day at work recently and that you are finding work fulfilling. This book will support you to continue on that path and make work even better for you.

If you answered 'no' to some or maybe even all of the above questions, then don't panic. This doesn't mean all is lost; it simply means it's the perfect time for positive change.

If you are not currently working, then this book will ensure that the next role is your best role yet. Whatever your situation, you will address and resolve issues which are holding you back, consider what changes you want to make, and be guided through the change with practical techniques. By the end of this book you will be fully equipped to be happy, healthy, safe and engaged at work.

Making change

Entering into any process of change can be daunting but making changes at work can feel particularly challenging, and clients often report to me that they feel trapped, unable to change their situation. This challenge contributes to feeling fed up at work. We don't like something, we're not happy, but it feels so hard to make changes – which begs the question, why?

Work is a very habitual process. Many of us go to work every day, or spend the majority of the week working, and so we often adapt to discomfort or habitual unhappiness without realizing we're doing so. We accept the daily grind, feeling a little more tired every day and feeling a gradual increase in stress, but it's subtle. Take starting a new commute. The first few weeks are exhausting but then we adapt. To be clear, the commute is no less exhausting; we just adjust to the exhaustion.

The impact is so creeping as to appear innocuous. We can tolerate an awful lot, and it's hard to recognize any negative consequences of the way we are working, until the situation reaches an extreme, or we take a deliberate step back to review.

When change is so subtle, we begin to question our ability to perform and cope because we don't feel we've changed, nor can we clearly see the increased pressure we are under. This further undermines our confidence and shakes our faith in our own decision-making. This lack of confidence keeps us feeling trapped. We blame ourselves.

We often have epiphanies when we are away on holiday because we finally have the headspace to think objectively about our situation. Sometimes these reflections prompt nothing more than an awareness and an intention to improve our routines, prioritize home life over work, and so on. But they can lead to more drastic decisions and change, and sometimes a fear of drastic change is enough to prevent reflection and keep us where we are. It's a vicious cycle.

We remain unhappy at work when we hold a belief that change has to be scary, dramatic and all encompassing. We believe that we cannot be happy in the existing role where we feel frustrated and unhappy and so we think we need to leave and get a new job and start over. This can bring with it many issues and impracticalities which, in turn, leave us feeling stuck.

Love it or leave it?

I've already expressed my disdain for the Instagram wisdom that tells you to 'love it or leave it'. Cute memes suggesting that you simply 'quit and be your own boss' are also unhelpfully muddying the waters. The inherent suggestion is that we are somehow failing if we are not in a position to uproot and set up a wildly successful business on our own. In reality, working for yourself is not a quick fix to unhappy workplace habits. You will carry your existing beliefs, structures and routines with you into your own business, too – only this time you will be on your own. You need to learn to be happy, healthy, safe and engaged in any role in order to truly be in a position to benefit from working for yourself or changing role.

I emphasize this point because you may be feeling a little nervous about reading this book in case it espouses big dramatic changes which don't feel applicable to or attainable by you right now. Please let that fear go. This book is about rebalancing. Bringing you back into the centre of your working day so that you can achieve everything you want to and feel true fulfilment at work. It's about creating a haven where you can be authentically you in the space where you will spend a significant part of your adult life. It is about ensuring that you feel happy and healthy in the workplace and that work supports and promotes your wider goals in life. This is about making work work for you, not the other way around.

People are often surprised when we discuss how awful their job is and I don't immediately tell them to run out of the door. But the reason I don't advocate a 'just quit' approach is because it doesn't work. You can quit as many jobs as you like but, if you have been unhappy in every single one of them, then, while it is possible that you have been unlucky, it is far more likely that there is an unaddressed issue. This will continue leading you directly to unhappiness in every role. The recurrence means that the honeymoon period for any new role will be shorter and the descent into unhappiness sharper and therefore all the more disappointing.

A terrible situation at work that has affected our self-esteem, knocked our confidence and generally diminished our health needs processing. It is naive to leave one job broken and expect another job to fix you. You need to establish your HHSE, build yourself up, and then consider what role you would like to do.

This way you are back in the driving seat. You are making decisions about where to go next and what role you want to do as opposed to your anxiety, stress, previous traumas or current fears making these decisions for you. Countless people leave jobs because they never learned the skills to be happy in the job they have. Truly happy. Not putting up with it. Not turning a blind eye. Not making do. Being truly happy at work. Sound too good to be true? Let's give it a go!

Being happy, healthy, safe and engaged at work

These four components – HHSE – underpin every wellbeing strategy I have ever developed, whether for a large global business, or for a self-employed homeworker. If one element is removed, then none of them works. You cannot be healthy if you are unsafe. You cannot be safe if you are disengaged. You cannot be happy if you are unhealthy. Each element, when working together to support the others, promises true wellness at work, regardless of the role you are in.

Even a small positive change in one area can have a significant improvement in the others, as they are all linked and all work together. The tools and tips provided throughout this book are going to teach you how to boost each of these fundamentals. Before we can begin to make changes, we need to understand the four components and establish your current HHSE score.

Happy

Being happy at work means exactly that: you experience feelings of happiness while at work. This also includes a sense of happiness when you think about your job and what you do for a living. This is about feeling happy to tell others what you do for work, seeing the greater purpose in your role and the place it holds in your life (beyond salary). Being happy at work does not mean that you won't have tough days or experience stress. But it does mean that, in spite of the tough days, the job itself supports your happiness.

The question 'Why be happy at work?' is an important one to consider. After all, isn't work just an exchange of money for services? No. Personally, I'm a passionate believer that we can and should be happy at work. The sheer amount of time that we spend at work is reason enough to seek happiness there. In a typical working week, we spend more time at work than we do with our friends, family and loved ones. We spend more time in our workplace than we do in our own bed. We'll spend more time in the workplace than we will travelling the world, taking time out, relaxing, pursuing hobbies and reading. In fact, we spend more time at work than we do anywhere else. This doesn't include the headspace that work will take up even when we aren't there and the subsidiary impacts of commuting, travel, planning etc.

Work doesn't stop when we shut the door and neither does the impact. If we have a bad day at work, it is hard to cleanly walk away from that. We will carry a challenging conversation or stressful situation home with us, packing it neatly into our bag as we prepare to leave for the day, travelling with it in the car or train, and then there it sits in our home, demanding our attention and distracting us from our relaxation.

This is even more the case if we work from home, where 42 per cent of us find it harder to separate out home and work. If there is no physical distance between us and work, then it is difficult to psychologically detach and walk away. Additionally, if we are working from home, then we need to consider that these stressful and difficult situations may now be taking place in our living rooms, our kitchens and at our dining tables. If home is no longer our safe sanctuary exclusively free of work and our space to relax, then where do we now escape to?

This is why we need and deserve to be happy at work and why happiness is such an important factor in our workplace wellbeing.

Healthy

There are two main factors to consider about health at work: the impact of work on our health, and the impact of our health on work.

Your work should not be negatively impacting your health, whether that's your psychological health because of too much stress and pressure, or your physical health through harm or injury. The impact of work should also not be felt outside work – for example, our roles shouldn't lead us to unhealthy behaviours such as stress-eating, unhealthy work–life boundaries or self-medication through alcohol.

Your health shouldn't be impacting work. In my line of work there is something called 'fitness to practise', and I have an obligation to my accrediting body to be physically and emotionally fit enough to do my job. This means that if there are circumstances in my life that may affect my work, I need to be mindful of them and aim to resolve them in order to be at my best for my clients. I believe we should all adopt fitness to practise principles in every role.

I have worked with employees who have very physically demanding jobs and they have been out drinking heavily the night before and are unable to complete their work the following day. Now we can all be guilty of the odd hangover from hell, but if you are consistently making choices which are not supportive of your work, or preventing you from being at your best, then you have to reconsider these choices. You need to be healthy at work in order to be happy, safe and engaged. Work should not negatively impact your health, and your health should not negatively impact your work.

When we feel healthy at work, we reap positive rewards. We feel more motivated, positive and focused on achieving our best. Being healthy at work also means that we are better able to handle the normal stresses of work, and thus a cycle is created where the healthier we *are* at work, the healthier we'll *be* at work.

A quick note on health *as* safety

When I present on health and wellbeing, I discuss health *as* safety, not health *and* safety, because, for me, they are inseparable. Often, companies want to know about their health and wellbeing data and they are confused when I tell them to look at their safety data. However, believe this to be true. Happy, healthy, safe and engaged employees do not have accidents.

Health issues *are* safety issues. Would you want to be a passenger on a train driven by a driver with fatigue? Or with low blood sugar? Poor decision-making can be attributed to an individual being hungry and fatigued. Research shows that if judges are hungry then you are less likely to be acquitted and more likely to receive a harsher sentence.[1] Doctors are more likely to prescribe antibiotics in the afternoon and less likely to focus on the holistic solutions they would have considered when they were less fatigued in the morning.[2] Health issues are safety issues, and the safety implications of unhealthy decisions are far reaching.

When we talk about our health at work we are talking about holistic health. Our health status impacts our work, and vice versa, every day, and we need to take care of it.

Safe

It is a given that you should be safe at work. No one should feel they are at risk in their workplace. Even in safety-critical roles where there can be an actual risk to life or significant risk of injury, every circumstance should be mitigated and every risk minimized wherever possible so that people feel confidently safe doing their job. We need to feel physically safe at work and not feel as though our workplace is compromising our safety.

We also need to be safe from psychological harm. We need to be allowed to innovate, create and even fail safely. We should be able to attend work free from bullying and harassment, stigma and stereotyping. Work shouldn't damage our physical or psychological health, and we should never feel unsafe when at work.

Engaged

Have you ever had one of those days where you are working on something that you are really interested in and excited by and before you know it you glance at your watch only to find that hours have passed by without you noticing? Isn't that an amazing feeling? You'll certainly know if you have had the opposite where you cannot get into the task you are meant to do and you keep clock watching, only to convince yourself that time is moving so slowly that it may actually be moving backwards. It's painful when we are not engaged in our work.

Being engaged at work means being mindfully involved in the task at hand. Ideally, you want to get into a flow state when working. This does not mean that every task is going to be fascinating and exciting, and of course we all have to spend some of our time on tasks that are less motivating or even downright boring. That's OK. You can still remain in an engaged state while engaged in a boring task.

How to assess your current happy, healthy, safe and engaged status

Regularly evaluating your HHSE status allows you to monitor change and the impacts of any new approaches that you take. This is a great activity to do when you start by stopping.

A word of warning, though: assessing your HHSE score can be a bit of a shock. Facing where we are can feel a little overwhelming, and your HHSE score may surprise you. It is not uncommon for people to score zero. Don't be put off. A lower than expected score is not a sign that you are doing anything wrong, nor that you are in the wrong career. But it is further evidence that we don't work with our wellbeing at the centre and work isn't set up to fulfil our full HHSE potential. The way we are currently working is not working for us, and we are not working well. It all needs to be reworked.

Activity: Assess your HHSE status

Read through the statements below and see which ones resonate with you. For every statement you agree with award yourself one point, then rate your status for each section out of 7.

Happy	/7	Healthy	/7	Safe	/7	Engaged	/7

Happy

1 I actively look forward to going to work

2 I am proud of the job that I do

3 The job I do gives me a daily sense of satisfaction

4 I smile when I think about my working day

5 If I didn't have to think about money, I would do the job I do for free

6 Given a choice of various roles, I would choose my job

7 I like talking about my job, my working day and my workplace

Healthy

1 I feel I can be at my best at work

2 I have clarity and clear thinking when I am at work

3 I make healthy choices at work

4 I am able to exercise as I want to during my working day

5 I make good food choices at work

6 I do not self-medicate through food and alcohol because of my job

7 Work does not negatively impact my mood, state of mind or cognitive ability

Safe

1 I am mindful of my physical safety at work

2 My bosses make decisions about my working hours with me in mind

3 I do not engage in unsafe workplace behaviours such as driving to work when tired

4 I am not distracted at work

5 I feel safe in my workplace, both physically and psychologically

6 I feel respected at work

7 I have clear work–life boundaries

Engaged

1 I can recall my last working day in detail

2 I understand the role my job plays in the wider company aims

3 I feel emotionally connected to my job

4 I take pride in my work

5 I find myself in a state of 'flow' where the time disappears

6 I am productive and focused at work

7 I feel mindful and present in my workplace

Review your score:

How did you do? For each section the scores reflect your status: $0–2$ = not; $3–5$ = somewhat; $6–7$ = very. For example, a score of $2/7$ for 'happy' suggests you are not happy at work.

Whatever your score, it is possible to be happy, healthy, safe and engaged at work and we'll begin seeing positive changes imminently. Don't be put off: approach the next stages with openness and curiosity.

Let the journey begin

When we start examining issues in detail, it may be that we draw attention to and highlight everything that is wrong with a situation and this can be challenging. It can be confronting to reassess a job you may have disengaged from, and it can raise awareness of issues that need addressing.

It is very normal for things to feel a little bit worse before they feel better, so don't give up. You will gain practical tips to get you through the bad bits, and create solutions so that you can become truly happy, healthy, safe and engaged, no matter where you are starting from.

Now you know where you are and what is possible, let's start the journey to get you there. Things are about to get a whole lot better.

Reworking starting

- Start by stopping.
- Check in with yourself, not those around you, when assessing how happy, healthy, safe and engaged you are at work.
- Health issues are safety issues, and it is important that we are healthy and safe at work.
- You don't need to leave your job to be happy at work – you can improve your current situation without making drastic changes.
- You now have your baseline HHSE score and can measure improvements in your health, happiness, safety and engagement in work.
- Things are about to get better.

3

Beyond Money to the True Value of Work

It's fair to say that when I ask people 'Why do you work?', there usually follows a sardonic look before they reply in a slow and deliberate voice: 'Because I have bills to pay.' Fair enough. But we know that we have to look beyond the money. One of the great workplace myths is that money is a marker of success. I appreciate, and have myself felt, the annoyance caused by someone talking about work not being about money when we have bills to pay and when money is our primary focus. I'm not telling you that money doesn't matter. It does. But it's not everything.

There are limitations to a purely money-focused mindset. Shifting our perspective supports our journey to be happy, healthy, safe and engaged, but it can be a hard shift to make. If you are currently in a role purely for the money, then changing your mindset is still useful, even if money remains your main reward for that role. In fact, a mindset shift could better support you financially. It's an odd twist that focusing on money can keep you poorer, both financially and emotionally. We'll explore shifting our mindset away from money and also how to survive in a job you are just doing for the money. We've all been there, and there are ways to protect your wellbeing even if you are in this situation.

Don't be turned off by the money talk. Money, and our reaction to it, is subjective, but whatever your situation, there are tools here to improve your workplace wellbeing.

Why is it about money in the first place?

Because we don't learn how to work, we grow up having conversations around arbitrary markers of success. Rather than putting ourselves and our values at the centre of our careers, let alone our health and happiness, we are instead encouraged to focus on money. This means we grow up confusing money with success, and consequently we often focus solely on salary.

A tale of success

When I told my partner that I was writing this book and specifically about this chapter he told me a story about a fisherman and a businessman which is well known but which was new to me. I'm going to retell it here because it is powerful.

A businessman sat overlooking a beach and noticed a fisherman who regularly returned to shore with a haul of large fish. Impressed, he asked the fisherman why he returned to shore so early, when he could obviously catch many more fish with his skill. The fisherman replied that he had plenty to feed his family and their guests. The businessman asked him what he did for the rest of the day, and he replied, 'I play with my children, I eat freshly cooked food, I relax, I swim and I spend time with my family.'

The businessman said, 'Listen to me. I'm an expert in business and I think I could really help you build an empire and be a success. First, you need to spend many more hours fishing, then eventually you will make enough money to have more boats and hire more fishermen to help you. From there you can organize much wider distribution, make a name for yourself, and establish worldwide success!'

The fisherman thought for a moment and said, 'Then what do I do?' The businessman smiled and said, 'You can do whatever you want! Retire early, spend your mornings fishing for pleasure and the rest of the day with your family, cooking, eating and swimming, enjoying the fruits of your labours.' The fisherman paused again and said, 'Isn't that what I am doing now?'[1]

Moving beyond a money mindset doesn't mean we forget the money or that we don't need money. It's about reconnecting us with the goals and values that will keep us happy, healthy, safe and engaged at work. To be clear, there is absolutely nothing wrong with wanting an abundant living. The majority of us go to work out of necessity, and it is a position of extreme privilege to be able to carry out a job or accept a role without first considering the salary. But it can't *just* be about the money. There is more value for us to gain from work than money alone.

HHSE boost: Reflection

Take a moment to mark where you are on the scale of money being important to you in your current role:

0 _____10

No importance   The sole reason

why I go to work

Money isn't everything

When we are focused solely on the money we earn, we often have to disregard or compromise on one of our core wellbeing areas. Often, people think they can stomach a lot in exchange for a salary, but the reality can feel very different. When you do a job that is disconnected from your values and which you struggle to engage in, you do not stay the same person while you work there.

Meet Jacob

When I started the job, it was a big hike in salary. I didn't really want the job, but I thought I would just do it for a year. It was a good incentive for me. I had a lot of debt, and money had been a worry for a long time, and I was really focused on earning more and giving myself a bit of breathing space. It just didn't work out how I thought it would. I really disliked the work, and I didn't enjoy what I was doing at all. I'd previously had a really hands-on role, and even though I didn't earn as much, I had a great team to work with. In this job I was in an office on my own. Sometimes the whole day would pass and I wouldn't see anyone. I wasn't really busy enough, but I didn't want to admit that, as I thought they might realize they didn't really need me, and I couldn't afford to lose my job.

I would hear my friends talking about how busy they were and really envy them. I kept thinking about all the work I could do and projects I could undertake, but I did nothing and eventually I just resented being there. No one ever checked up on my work; no one even seemed to notice if I was there or not. How are you meant to stay motivated when a cardboard cut-out of you would have the same

> interaction? I was bored and a bit depressed. Yes, I was
> earning good money, but once I paid off a few cards,
> I didn't even really notice the money. I felt so ungrateful
> because the me of a year ago, anxious and in debt, would
> have killed to be earning more, but now I was earning more,
> I just felt unhappy and unfulfilled. I also felt really trapped.
> I knew that, if I stayed, I could clear my debt completely
> in five years. I used to sit there and calculate the exact
> day I could be debt free and then resign. But then I found
> I spent more money on things to get me through my day, or
> because I was bored, and so my debt repayments slowed.
> Before I knew it, I wasn't really making any headway, I felt as
> though I'd failed, and I felt stuck. I didn't think I'd earn this
> anywhere else. I didn't want to stay. I couldn't leave. I didn't
> really recognize myself anymore.

Research backs Jacob's experience, as studies have shown that financial incentives without clear role expectations have a negative effect on performance and demotivate us.[2] Workplace perks and financial incentives will only be felt once and will result in a very short-term and unsustainable boost.[3] This means you cannot build a meaningful relationship with work based on the benefits package alone. You simply stop feeling it. Free gym membership and a generous bonus are fantastic perks to begin with, but even the most mindful and grateful employee will stop seeing these as extras and start to see these as the norm. This means you have to look beyond the salary towards what work really means and can provide for you.

More money may make your life a little easier month to month, but if you are feeling dissatisfied and unhappy at work, it will not solve your problems. Money cannot solve your problems, because money isn't the problem. A money mindset is. When we focus on money alone, we assume we are unhappy with our salary and seek better payment while ignoring what is really happening in work. If you are in a situation like Jacob, and you have debt to repay and you need the money, then looking beyond the money is still useful. It can provide a vision and purpose and further incentive to start making work work for you.

Potential for growth

When the American business executive and philanthropist Sheryl Sandberg left Google to move to Facebook, she was advised against it. After all, it would mean that she would be taking a substantial pay cut. But Sandberg wasn't interested in salary alone. She was interested in the potential for growth. It is this potential for growth that has allowed her to soar in her career and do what she loves, within an atmosphere she thrives in, while earning more than she ever has.[4] It is a position of privilege to be able to take a pay cut, but potential for growth is something we should all look for in every role we have.

When we are solely salary-focused, we often miss out on or ignore opportunities for personal development. These are the opportunities that will expand our skillset, allow us to explore new avenues and, ultimately, lead us to experience greater happiness at work. Moreover, focusing on growth and self-development gives you options and pathways that money can't offer. Money only gives you money back. Money doesn't feed your creativity or help you to grow. It won't let you develop and move on to higher or better things, which also means you won't earn more. Ironically, focusing on money, long term, makes you poorer.

Looking beyond your salary empowers you to take chances, grab opportunities, focus on doing what you love, not just

what pays the bills. This is about opening your mindset
to the many and varied opportunities that exist for you at
work right now. You don't need to walk out of the door into
something new, you can focus your energy on experiences
that build your creativity, your confidence and your passion.

OK, I will change my mindset, but for now I need the money

We all have times where we work in a role solely to pay the
bills. That's the very nature of work and the economy we live
in, and that's OK. We do what we need to do. But we can
lose sight of our wellbeing in these roles, as we dismiss them
as short-term and 'just for now'. However, we can continue
to grow and boost our happy, healthy, safe and engaged scores
even in a role that isn't obviously going to do so. Below are
some tips for staying sane when working solely for the money.

Tip 1: Put a time limit on it

If we take a job that we know is not right for us long term,
then we need to put a time limit on it. This is a clearly
defined period of time in which we are willing to work in
this job, but no longer. We don't have to share that time limit
with anyone (and definitely not with our boss!), but we hold
the limit in mind nonetheless. Knowing that we are giving
this job one year or two years (or longer if needed, as long
as it's clearly defined), while we get things in order, stops us
feeling trapped and gives the role a new sense of purpose.
This isn't a forever role. It's important to keep that in mind.

Situations feel very different when we know they are
temporary. When I've been unhappy in roles, putting a time

limit on it has taken a weight off me. It's as though you can see the finish line. Remember how our brain loves a plan? Even if it's not an immediate win, having an end in sight supports our wellbeing in roles we are not enjoying. Also, we can use our time limit to keep ourselves honest and motivated about progress. If we give a role two years and after 18 months we haven't made any steps to change or progress, then we can start thinking, 'OK, I have six months left, what do I want to do?' I don't recommend waiting that long, though, there is huge power in consistent and regular reflection, and it will keep us to time.

Tip 2: Make a plan

To complement your time limit, make a plan. I don't mean a vague notion or idea type of plan. I mean an actual written-down, thought-through, able-to-describe-it-to-someone-else plan. If we are in a job for the money alone, then what is the plan? What are we doing with the money? How long are we doing this for? By writing out our next steps and planning, we will feel more empowered, and less as though we just need to grit our teeth and get on with it.

Tip 3: Look for the opportunities and perks

We can immediately disengage from a for-the-money job, and this means we miss out on what it potentially offers us. We need to make ourselves familiar with every perk and benefit that the company we are working for offers. Almost all companies have an employee assistance programme (EAP) which allows employees free access to help, support and guidance in many different areas of their lives. These include finance and debt management, childcare, legal issues and even basic counselling. However, the average EAP uptake by employees in the UK is only 5 per cent.[5] Companies of all sizes often link with high-street chains to secure discounts on clothes and food. There might be a cycle to work scheme in place which could allow us to buy a new bike at a reduced price and spreading the cost. Again, these are initiatives which are sorely underused, despite being free for employees to take advantage of. Take time to explore what work can offer outside the workplace, even in the short term.

Tip 4: Reward yourself – often!

Rewards don't need to be big or expensive, but they are most effective when they are frequent, consistent and something we really desire. If we are tolerating, rather than enjoying, a job at the moment, then we need to inject moments of joy into our day. This means prioritizing rewards.

Humans are behavioural creatures, and having regular rewards keeps us motivated and engaged, which is essential for our wellbeing at work. A reward could be something as simple as a short walk in the sunshine on our lunch break, taking time to read a book by our favourite author, or catching up with a friend.

A job that isn't intrinsically rewarding can lead us to feel low in mood, and so it is really important to counter that and purposefully build our own engagement and happiness into the working day.

Tip 5: Challenge unhelpful beliefs about this role

Challenge anything that isn't supporting your health and happiness in this role. If we spend every day thinking, 'I hate this job', 'I can't believe I'm having to work here' or 'I'm stuck here', then we need to challenge those thoughts and reframe the situation. I like honesty in my reflections so I would recommend a reframe along the lines of 'This role isn't perfect, but it is serving a purpose. I am proud of myself for using this role to serve my needs. I will not work here for ever.' It's not about trying to kid yourself that everything is perfect, but a balanced reflection is going to be better for your mood than managing a toxic and negative mindset every day.

A simple mantra or mindset shift to combat negative thoughts is really helpful to reconnect us to the purpose of this role. Remember the myth about work being our identity? This is where reframing can be so helpful. We are so much more than our role and our work. Try to reconnect with who you are.

Tip 6: Connect to your ikigai

I have long been fascinated by the Japanese concept of *ikigai*. Sadly, this has been somewhat oversimplified, and if you google ikigai, you will typically see a Venn diagram linking the phases 'What you love', 'What the world needs', 'What you are good at' and 'What you can get paid for'. Right there in the middle you find your ikigai. However, ikigai, like so many beautiful Japanese concepts, is far richer than that.

True ikigai refers to our purpose, our reason for being, our life's work. It is what gets us up in the morning. Rather than being defined as a single role, it is the *value* of what matters most to us, and the lifetime pursuit of it. Ikigai is not financially driven. It is not driving you towards an end game because, for the Japanese, there is no end game. There is no concept of retirement when it comes to ikigai. Instead, you uncover your life's purpose and you connect with that purpose every day. What an incredibly powerful tool to bring joy into your life, and indeed, your workplace.

Let's say, for example, that your ikigai is to help people. That's what you love, that's what gets you up in the morning, that's what helps you feel good and what supports your wider goals and values in life. You can achieve your ikigai every day, even in a just-for-the-money job, by actively seeking out opportunities that allow you to help others.

This daily pursuit can support you to feel more like yourself and help you find meaning and enjoyment. It's a powerful source of joy and empowerment, and it connects you to the values that matter the most to you.

HHSE boost: Reflection

Take a moment and reflect on the below:

- What makes you feel good?
- What matters to you?
- What sets your soul alight?
- What makes you happy?
- What would you describe your ikigai as (even if you don't have it exactly figured out yet)?

Even if there isn't a perfect match between what we'd like to do and our current role, we can take the value or meaning of our ikigai and seek opportunities to apply it. We can recognize ways in which our role already serves us and identify any gaps that need our attention and energy. We go from being passive, stressed and frustrated, to active and truly alive in our workplace.

Tip 7: Continually check in

The biggest issue with a for-the-money job is that we disengage from it. We need to regularly check in to bring ourselves back to our goals, our values, our plan and our purpose. Start by stopping regularly, daily if need be, to see how you are feeling and what you may need to support yourself at this time. You may be thinking, 'Urgh, I don't have time for all this reflection and thinking in among my working day.' There is a wonderful saying that everyone should meditate for twenty minutes per day, unless they don't have time, in which case they should meditate for an hour. The point being, if you don't have time to protect and boost your wellbeing, then there is something wrong with your day. Even five minutes at the start of your shift or on a coffee break can make a huge difference. Invest the time in yourself to check in on how work is working for you, and what you need next.

Solo earning

When we work for ourselves, money takes on a very different feel and can impact our HHSE scores. Unlike working for a salary, when you work for yourself, you lose the stability of a regular income, which can cause us to be fearful about future earnings. If you have an off-day, a demotivated day, or an unproductive day in a regular paid role then you get paid regardless. However, when you work for yourself then you need to do the work or you won't get paid. Even if you make a decent income as a solo worker, there will be periods where you don't earn as much, either because a contract falls through or a project gets pushed back, and those months where you watch your savings deplete can be very scary.

This fear of not making enough money can prevent us from prioritizing our health and happiness. Ironically, many of us choose to work for ourselves in order to have more work-free time, and yet money fears can trap us into more work than ever. We may not take vacations, or time out at weekends, because we feel we have to be hustling and earning every second that we can. We see vacations as time where we don't earn, rather than periods of necessary rest and recharge. This can be detrimental to our own happiness but also to the happiness of those around us (partners of the self-employed have to be particularly patient!). But there are some ways of managing our fears about money and being self-employed which will increase our HHSE and prevent us getting caught in a money–worry trap.

- **Learn what you are doing.** There are many courses available which will take you through business finance, what you can and can't put down as an expense, the information your invoices need to include, and so on. In fact, many banks and local government schemes offer these courses for free. By learning what you are doing, you take the fear out of managing your money, leaving you in better control. Also, you'll get a good idea of how much you need to put aside for your tax bill, which saves a lot of stress later on!

- **Know your worth.** Self-employed workers often underestimate or undervalue their work, so it's important to pitch yourself at the right price. There's no point putting in the lowest bid to get the work if you then resent all the hours you are putting in for minimum wage. Do your research, find out what the going rate is, and make sure you reflect that in your prices.

- **Don't take it personally.** Seventy per cent of self-employed individuals will struggle to get paid at some point.[6] This can feel scary and overwhelming, but it's so important to remember this isn't personal. It's usually the consequence of overcomplicated finance departments in large companies and it's easily resolved, as long as you stay calm. Get clear on your client's payment terms and when you can expect payment. Invoice regularly and on time, stating your payment terms on every invoice. Don't forget to chase payment. Consider having a separate email address for the finance side of things, even if you manage it yourself. By separating out your identity you can be stronger in your finance emails than if you are trying to maintain a good client relationship. You can even drop in something like 'My finance team mentioned they hadn't received payment?' to your client to prompt them.

- **Stay organized.** Keeping track of money is much easier if we do it regularly. A half-hour in the diary every week to log income and expenses can save you real heartache and stress when it comes to submitting your company accounts. It's tempting to push it aside and focus solely on the work, but you will thank your past self for their diligence when you are not staying up late frantically looking for receipts or trying to remember when you invoiced someone just ahead of tax submission deadlines. Little and often is the way to prevent money fears ruining your HHSE score.

- **Don't accept work you don't want to do**, if you can possibly avoid it. Just because you can help someone doesn't mean you have to. Don't get pulled into work that isn't yours to do, or that you don't care about. Remember you chose to work for yourself for many reasons, including better happiness. Honour that intention.

Whether working for ourselves or someone else, freeing ourselves from a money mindset and looking to the greater value of work protects our health and wellbeing. Success is not measured in pounds or dollars, and we need to connect with the true value of our work, the opportunities work can offer us, and how we can use work to gain happiness, health, safety and engagement. Money blocks our path to HHSE, and shifting our mindset beyond money opens up all manner of opportunities. Start thinking about the true value of your own work, and how you deserve so much more than money.

Reworking money

- You don't need to quit your job, but you do need to quit your money mindset.
- Focusing on money can, in the longer term, leave us financially poorer.
- It's important to regularly reward ourselves when we are in jobs that we don't find intrinsically rewarding.
- Focusing on your ikigai moves you past money and reconnects you with your true values.
- Working for yourself can change your relationship with money – take control with simple steps in order to avoid fear-based decisions.

4

Do No Harm

Have you ever noticed that when you need it the least is exactly when you are most likely to experience life's little annoyances? You know how it is: you have a lot on your mind and are spinning multiple plates and OUCH! You shut your hand in your car door. Or maybe you are rushing to get out of the door and you stub your toe on the same piece of furniture that you breeze past every single day. What the heck?! A pile of papers to get through sits on your desk, and you knock your coffee over it. This is not coincidence. There is a good neurological explanation for these painful irritations, and the root cause can be work.

The basic principle of any workplace should be that people don't get hurt. I call this the 'do no harm' principle. Your workplace shouldn't harm you, and you shouldn't harm your workplace. It is a contract of mutual protection and respect. To actualize this principle, we have to be mindful of the multiple safety risks we face every day at work.

Health and safety laws, rules and regulations mean that many of us assume that we are safe at work. Indeed, if you work in an office environment, then you may never have thought about your personal safety, beyond tripping over a cable or a colleague's laptop bag.

There are, however, many reasons why we need to pay attention to our safety at work. We need to recognize not just our physical safety but our psychological and emotional safety. It is only by being aware of potential risks that we can mitigate them.

Health *as* safety

For many years now I have emphasized 'health *as* safety' as opposed to health *and* safety. Health issues are safety issues, and we cannot separate them. As we become aware of the impact that work can have on our health, and vice versa, we can begin to re-evaluate our role. Are we making choices that support us to be safe at work? Is work allowing us to be our healthiest and safest self, both physically and psychologically? Remember the basic principle: you shouldn't be harming work and work shouldn't be harming you. If this isn't the case, then this needs to be addressed.

Would you notice if work was affecting your health?

If I asked you, 'How does work affect your health day-to-day?', what would you tell me? Often people focus on the extremes. 'I was so stressed I didn't sleep well all of last week' or 'I got promoted and went out all weekend – my head still hurts from the hangover!'

We notice the boost to our mental health when we are absolutely buzzing after a brilliant day: we got a thank-you email from our boss, we closed that important deal, or met a customer's exacting demands. The sense of satisfaction and wellbeing we get from a great day at work can be hard to rival.

Similarly, a disastrous day at work is hard to ignore. A day where everything went wrong, where we felt we failed, where we were left feeling uncertain, angry or disappointed, is one we carry with us for the rest of the week and beyond.

So why do we only pay attention to how we feel at the extremes?

The truth is that day in, day out we can become mindless at work. We stop tuning in to situations and stop meaningfully engaging in our work, as we fall into the autopilot of a work–eat–sleep–repeat mentality. This means we not only miss out on all the positives, but we don't see the red flags and warning signs that are telling us we are approaching our own danger zone for our physical and mental health and safety.

This is where harm can happen. It sneaks up on us while we are busy paying attention elsewhere. We often ignore the gentle warnings because we are simply too busy, overloaded and stressed to realize that we are busy, overloaded and stressed! This also holds true for positive interactions, and we miss the cues highlighting what lights us up and makes us feel good. We rush past the small triumphs and victories that would connect us with our values, and miss seeing the synergy between those values and our role.

Work can affect us every day, but we don't tune into the daily impact. Our state of autopilot in the workplace does not boost our HHSE score. Moving past our signals at pace and not seeing the path we are on means that we end up at an uncomfortable destination without understanding how we got there. We have taken on additional duties, are responsible for a new task, or are struggling with a difficult client whom no one else wanted. We may also be missing out on opportunities that we did want, having not recognized the cues and pointers that were telling us that this would be a good path for us to follow.

Crying over spilt milk … or coffee

Let's get back to why you knocked your coffee all over your desk, and why life seems to be at its most challenging when we just need it to run smoothly. To understand this, we turn to the hippocampus. The hippocampus forms an integral part of your brain's function. Associated with learning and memory, your hippocampus is responsible for filing and sorting in the brain. It also creates and stores memories such as your last blissful beach getaway. We have a lot to thank our hippocampus for.

Our hippocampus is a multitasker, and so as well as storing those holiday memories, it places you where you are in the world. Literally. Within the hippocampus are place and grid cells which interact with each other to decipher exactly where you are in the world, and help to place you in relation to other objects and people.[1] If you remember graph paper from school, then you'll remember an entire page laid out in front of you constructed of tiny squares. Now imagine those squares as triangles and that's how your hippocampus sees the world around you, and this is the map it uses to accurately place you within your surroundings.

When we experience stress, our body's natural stress response impacts the function of the hippocampus. We'll examine your stress response more closely in Chapter 6, but for now, know that your impacted hippocampus struggles to place you precisely where you are in the world. Hence why, when you are feeling stressed and overwhelmed, you may misjudge the edge of a table and spill your coffee or misjudge the edge of your bed and hop around clutching your poor stubbed toe. It is no coincidence that when we are stressed, the number of daily annoyances we face increases.

There are safety-critical implications of not being able to place ourselves accurately in the world. Workers who experience higher levels of stress are at increased risk of accidents compared to those with lower levels.[2] If we operate heavy or sharp machinery and cannot accurately place where our fingers are in relation to the sharp parts, then we could be in real trouble. For the same reason, you should never jump into your car when you are in a very stressed state. At best you may just hit your tyre on a curb, but at worst you could misjudge something serious and cause a fatal accident.

The hippocampus isn't the only part responsible for causing some mishaps. When we are in a state of heightened stress, our brains can start operating under amygdala hijack. When our amygdala is in charge, we are far more likely to engage in risk-taking behaviour. Again, a little extra stress at work could be the difference between running an amber light or waiting patiently at the junction.

There are many elements of our day-to-day working life that we never think about but we must learn to tune in to boost our HHSE scores. We cannot ignore the potential risks which we face. Even something as innocent as sitting quietly at your desk can pose a safety risk.

Are you sitting comfortably?

For a long time, seating arrangements have been a source of debate in the workplace. It is exceptionally difficult to find an office chair that suits everyone, and hell hath no fury like a colleague who has had their 'special chair' settings messed with. But there is more to your posture than merely being comfortable.

If someone were to run at us (as though they were going to attack us), our body's natural instinct would be to curl in on itself. This wouldn't be a carefully considered choice; this would be instinctively how our bodies would react, because they have detected a threat and so the brain's instinct is to protect our internal organs. Consider that posture: arms folded in front of us, head down, muscles braced and tense, rounded back and shoulders – essentially as close as we can get to curling into a tight ball.

Now consider how you sit at your laptop. What cues are you sending your brain? Rounded shoulders as you reach for the keyboard. Dropped head in line with the screen. Arms folded awkwardly across your body as you fight for table space or elbow room. Although less dramatic than the full-on curled-up-in-a-ball protective stance, our laptop posture tells our brain that we are under threat. When we sit in this way at our computers, in meetings, in challenging or uncomfortable situations at work, we continually tell our brains that we are in danger.

Imagine that. Something as simple as sitting at our laptop with a defensive posture could be wiring our brain to perceive our laptop as a threat. This could go some way to understanding that indefinable sense of dread or stress we feel when we even picture ourselves at work. Perhaps we aren't dreading the contents of our inbox, but even so our brain has associated that inbox with threat.

This is worth paying attention to because continuously activating your stress and threat responses, for no good reason, is not good for your health. Also, having a negative association with your laptop is not ideal, and certainly not motivational.

Our bodies tell our brains how to react and vice versa. This applies to our mood state as well. Away from a laptop, any work environment can be impacted by your posture. How do you spot an engaging, high-energy leader on a factory floor? By the way they are standing. They are not slouching, hands in pockets, head down, avoiding eye contact. They are moving around at pace, being open and approachable, greeting and connecting with others. They convey all of this through their body language.

Sitting or standing up straight has been proven to enhance motivation, optimism and productivity. When we stand tall, we make better decisions, feel more positive and are protected from a dip in mood. All of this, just from our physical stance.

This is why power postures are so, well, powerful! Sitting or standing tall, with your arms relaxed by your sides, a good solid stance with no protection or defensiveness, tells your brain that you have got this situation under control, and guess what? Your brain believes you. Instead of spiralling, you will be reviewing your emails or demands from a place of calm confidence, ready to overcome any challenges. The simplest way to turn your whole working day around? Check your posture.

HHSE boost: Posture

Set a reminder every hour to check in with your posture and stand with confidence for an instant mood boost. Monitor how you feel throughout your working day as a result.

Catching your breath

Linda Stone, a writer, researcher and former executive at Apple and Microsoft, discovered a new phenomenon she labelled 'email apnoea'. Stone found that around 80 per cent of people unconsciously hold their breath, or breathe shallowly, when responding to email or working at screens.[3] With the average employee spending 28 per cent of their working week on email, sending and receiving around 620 emails per week,[4] that is an awful lot of time spent holding your breath.

Research by Dr Margaret Chesney and Dr David Anderson at the US National Institutes of Health (NIH) demonstrated that holding one's breath contributes to stress-related diseases, and disturbs the body's balance of oxygen, carbon dioxide and nitric oxide. These are essential to keeping our immune system balanced and strong enough to fight infection, and reduce inflammation. Shallow breathing can also trigger a sympathetic nervous system 'fight or flight' response. If we stay in this state of emergency breathing and hyperarousal for extended periods of time, it can not only impact sleep, memory and learning, but also exacerbate existing anxiety and depression.

Would you ever have thought that sitting at your desk reading your email could pose a health and safety risk? This is why we need to learn how to work. Imagine if you'd been taught this at school. How differently you would have entered the workplace if you'd been armed with more awareness! This is why it is so important that we tune in and recognize how work may be affecting our health and safety, without us even realizing. It is possible that, without paying attention and mitigating the impact, something as simple as answering emails could be making us sick.

If we consider how well we feel following a holiday, is it possible that one of the biggest differences between work and home is that we are simply free to breathe? If we widen these implications to outside the workplace, does this explain some of the negative impact of our tech addiction and constant screen time? It's certainly food for thought.

HHSE boost: Breathing

Pay attention to your breath and consciously take some slow, deep breaths as you complete screen work. Monitor the impact on your mood and your working day overall.

Working on your energy

Another impact work may have without you noticing could be a change in your mood or mental state. Sometimes we may need those around us to help us identify this one – if they are feeling brave! Our partners and friends may see that we are short-tempered, more abrasive and less capable of making a decision after work. Perhaps our mood darkens after we've glanced at a work email. Perhaps work makes us more impulsive and our risk profile changes, meaning we drink more heavily or spend more money than usual. It's not uncommon for work stress to lead to some serious shopping. The misnomer 'retail therapy' leads people to see shopping as a solution to low mood states. Research found that 62 per cent of purchases had been made in an attempt to lift the mood of the shopper.[5] While this is fine when money is available, it can mask a wider issue that needs addressing, and becomes problematic if it leads to regular or compulsive shopping and money is tight.

Often, we know when work has caused us to be stressed as we swear and mutter our way through the day, or our face hurts from maintaining the rictus grin in a valiant effort not to show our true feelings. We can be less tuned into the subtler impacts of work, such as a diminishment of motivation, a struggle to focus or concentrate, less engagement with friends and family and increased isolation. We may not notice how work is leaving us little energy for anything else in our lives, and so the space it occupies becomes disproportionately important. We can become entangled in a vicious cycle, where we are being softly drained by work and have no capacity to engage in activities that would energize us. In this way, work may prevent us making better decisions about our health and wellbeing.

It is so important that we are alert to the impact that work can have on our safety, and why the impact of work on health goes far beyond accidents and statistics. There are many subtle layers to the 'do no harm' principle, and it is only by understanding each layer that we can truly be happy, healthy, safe and engaged at work.

A bad day at work example

A bad day at work can be defined as a day which has a negative impact on us, be it psychological or physical, or both. We'll be exploring more of our stress response and why the physiological impacts occur, but for now let's spot the health and safety risks as they happen. Let's work through a bad day at work which, in this case, will start the night before.

You get into bed and find that you are tired but wired. In other words, you find it difficult to shut your brain off and get to sleep. (That will be all the adrenaline and noradrenaline in your system.) This leaves you feeling as though your brain is a hamster on a wheel. You want to shut down and go to sleep but you can't stop your thoughts going around and around.

You have a restless night, mindful of the minutes ticking down until you have to get up. You worry that tomorrow will be harder and more challenging because you haven't slept, thinking 'I am too tired to have a good day at work' (negative mindset). You become increasingly agitated by the lack of sleep, meaning that, when you do eventually get up, you are exhausted. You get up feeling vaguely harassed. There is nothing you can put your finger on, but you just feel a bit off. Your partner wishes you a great day at work, and a sarcastic inner voice snorts and thinks, 'Yeah right!' (You dismiss your partner's good wishes, which can lead to disconnection in your relationship.) You put an extra spoon of coffee into your mug because you are going to need that caffeine today! (An unhealthy decision that will impact your mood for the entire day.)

You get into your car and annoyingly you bump your knee hard on the steering wheel. (That'll be the lack of sleep and an overwhelmed hippocampus.) You rub your sore knee and mutter. You notice that bumping your knee caused you to jolt your arm, and you've splashed coffee onto your trousers. Never mind. You don't care enough to go back into the house and change. (Tiredness and low mood often cause a temporary lack of care in your personal appearance.)

You drive to work and some idiot cuts you up in traffic (a negative perception of others). You beep and mouth a choice word or two at them (risk-taking behaviour), then feel your heart rate quicken as you pull up behind them at the traffic lights – are they going to get out? Thankfully no – they pull away, but you arrive at the office feeling a little shaky from adrenaline, caffeine and pain. You feel depleted even before you've got to your workplace.

You open your emails and immediately scan for the 'screamers'. (Our brain only scans for threat and we have to train it to pay equal attention to the positives.) You see an invite to a 6 p.m. meeting for a project that you are really interested in, but honestly, you're tired and you don't think you have the energy to stay late (disengagement from your goals, values and interests). You are about to reply with an explanation but get asked to jump onto an important call and so you hit decline on the invite and jump on the call (you're acting against your values – you would have liked to offer an explanation for not attending the meeting). The call is both uninteresting and not urgent and you resent the time you spend on it. You are grumpy and fed up by the time you finish (impacted mood).

You have so much to do today that you cannot prioritize, and so despite working your socks off all day, you feel you don't actually achieve anything. You are in back-to-back meetings, so you nip down to the on-site coffee shop to grab a sandwich and a bag of crisps which you eat walking back to your desk (unhealthy and rushed choices). You feel bloated and uncomfortable (inflammation) and oh so tired that you grab another coffee (reliance on caffeine). Lack of sleep is really catching up with you. Luckily, it's Shamir's birthday and he brought in cake for the office so you grab two pieces to give you the sugar boost you need to get through the afternoon (unhealthy choices). That's better! Now you are perked up and ready for the last of your afternoon meetings.

You smile at a colleague as they walk past your desk, but they don't smile back. 'What's their problem?' you think, confused and hurt by their attitude. (This is the same colleague who worked really hard to get you on the 6 p.m. invite that you declined with no explanation. No wonder they didn't smile back at you!)

That's it. You've had enough of this day, and so you pack up and head back to the car. You notice when you get to the car that your chest feels a little tight (shallow breathing). 'My word, I'm unfit,' you think as you throw your things onto the passenger seat. Your bag falls into the footwell and the contents spill out (impacted spatial awareness). The perfect end to a rubbish day. You drive past your gym and look the other way – no one has the time or energy for that tonight (disruption of goals and values). You get home and glance at the fridge as you pour yourself a large glass of wine. You have your New Year resolutions pinned to the fridge door which include no drinking alcohol during the week, exercising five days per week, and doing something good for your career. You roll your eyes and head to the sofa, wine in hand, and watch Netflix (amygdala hijack). It'll be bedtime soon. Hopefully you'll sleep better tonight. (External locus of control – your behaviour is not setting you up for a good night's sleep, and just 'hoping' for one won't benefit you.)

Wowsers – what a day! What really stands out about this day at work is that … it doesn't stand out. It is a standard, if slightly annoying, day and we have probably all experienced something similar. However, we can see this is a harmful day, which leads to the question: What if it's not a one off? What if, day in, day out, you are not sleeping well, not making decisions that support your values and your goals, not able to focus on what you want to achieve? What is that doing to your overall HHSE and how can you prevent the negative impact?

Activity: Reflect on a bad day at work

Take yourself through the last day at work which didn't feel great. It may have been today, it may have been recently, or it may have been a particularly bad day that sticks in your memory. Reflect on the questions below to ascertain the impact that a bad day at work has on you personally:

1 How did you sleep the night before?

2 Did you wake feeling rested, or were you still feeling tired?

3 How did you feel as you got out of bed? Did you feel energized and motivated, or did you feel as though you were dragging yourself out of bed?

4 Did you encounter any annoyances either in the home or on your commute to work?

5 Looking back on that day, can you see any positives?

6 Did you notice the positives at the time or were they overshadowed by negative events?

7 How did people treat you? How did you treat other people?

8 Did you achieve everything you wanted to that day?

9 What mood were you in when leaving work? What did you notice in your body physically and emotionally?

10 Did your behaviour after work align with your values/goals?

Using the above questions as reflective touchstones allows you to understand where work may be having a negative impact on you. It may be that all goes really well and you set yourself up with good intentions for the day ahead, but it all falls apart when you arrive at work. What is holding you back from having a truly great day at work? What can you do about this?

Reflecting on the 'do no harm' principle, we have highlighted many ways that you could be harming work and work could be harming you, and we can see how quickly we are drawn into a vicious cycle, which impacts both our psychological and our physical health. As we've seen, the results of a bad day at work do not just affect us in the workplace. The impacts continue to affect us and cause unhealthy behaviours and actions outside the workplace.

These examples look at our physical health and safety and the impact that can be felt on our mood, but what about psychological safety? The next chapter will focus on the psychological safety factors that we need to be considering in our everyday work day.

Reworking physical safety

- Health issues are safety issues.
- Our work impacts our physical health and safety.
- Without paying attention we can miss both the positive and the negative cues which can support us to make decisions leading to a happier and healthier self.
- Paying deliberate attention to our posture and the way that we breathe can mitigate day-to-day work stresses which we may not even be aware of.
- Small changes can make a big difference to our safety and mitigate daily risks at work.

5

Psychological Safety

'You need a better name for this,' my colleague Paul said, gulping a coffee as we walked up to the safety review meeting. I'd been called in to debrief his team after a serious, but thankfully not fatal, incident on his factory floor. 'I mean, I get it,' he continued, 'but should we really be bringing anything "psychological" into the workplace?'

My response?

'Yes.'

Psychological and physical safety are inextricably linked, and both impact us at work. The same 'do no harm' principle applies to psychological safety as to physical safety. Work shouldn't harm you, and you shouldn't harm work. But what is our psychological safety, and how does it tie into the four pillars of workplace wellbeing?

Professor Amy Edmondson from Harvard Business School coined the term 'psychological safety' and describes it as 'a belief that one will not be punished or humiliated for speaking up with ideas, questions, concerns or mistakes'. When it comes to the workplace, Edmondson describes the necessity of psychological safety, insisting that 'a sense of confidence that the team will not embarrass, reject or punish someone for speaking up' is needed. Edmondson also states that psychologically safe teams require 'interpersonal trust and mutual respect' in order to be successful.[1] In other words, you need to know that you can speak up at work without your colleagues humiliating or rejecting you.

One can immediately see the benefits, and it isn't a lot to ask, but realistically how many of us speak up or challenge an idea, or someone's approach, at work? How comfortable are we telling someone that we think what they are doing is wrong? How open are the people around us to being challenged? How open are we ourselves to being critiqued or questioned about the way we work? Do we welcome suggestions of different and better ways to complete our work?

A lack of willingness to embrace others' viewpoints and challenges to the way we are working may go some way to explaining the continued lack of equality we see across the workforce. We continually see people hiring and promoting those of the perceived same gender, race, education level and socio-economic status as them. Unconscious bias may lead us to look for points of similarity in people we hire because similarities make us feel safer.[2] We are more likely to see this inequality in jobs and sectors where leaders are not promoting psychological safety, or are unwilling to be challenged and therefore don't embrace new ideas, a diverse team or challenges to the 'status quo'. Inevitably, this has impacts for development, diversity of thought, creativity and innovation within teams, as well as continually blocking progression for those who are 'other' to those hiring. Psychological safety has far-reaching consequences and is more complex than it first appears.

There are four stages of psychological safety.[3] These are:

1 **Inclusion safety** – we want to belong and connect with others. There is a basic human need to be part of the gang, and we want to feel as though we are accepted and included by others. This is more than seeking friendship; this is an evolutionary development in the brain to ensure survival. When we experience social rejection the pain centres of the brain are activated – being rejected by others is literally painful. This means that we strive to be included and belong and we want to do so securely, without feeling at risk of being excluded. We want to be accepted for who we are.

2 **Learner safety** – we want to grow, learn and develop. We want to be able to question, try out new things, feel encouraged to explore and see what works for us, and receive constructive and helpful feedback for our development. Have you ever nodded along in a discussion with no clue what anyone else is talking about, all the while praying hard that no one turns to you and asks, 'What do you think?'? A lack of learner safety means we shut down, won't ask questions, even if we don't understand something, and are also less likely to be open and vulnerable with others, as it just won't feel safe.

3 **Contributor safety** – we want to make a difference. Being able to contribute and watch our ideas take shape is extremely satisfying. We need to be able to reach our potential, without feeling overlooked or as though we are not trusted in our roles. If we don't have contributor safety, then we won't join in as our ideas and inputs will feel disregarded and ignored. A lack of contributor safety can be extremely demotivating, prevent personal growth and leave us feeling unfulfilled.

4 **Challenger safety** – we want to be able to change a process or a behaviour and make it better. Challenger safety allows us to challenge the way a task or process is being done, or the way an idea is being communicated. It is an essential safety component, as we need to feel safe to challenge if we see something dangerous or believe that there is inherent risk in someone's actions. Challenger safety protects us from feeling vulnerable and also helps us to avoid conflict as those around us are open and prepared to listen to our questions, rather than become defensive and try to shut the conversation down. A lack of challenger safety is often the most uncomfortable to experience in the workplace, as it can leave us in a position where we don't feel safe, either psychologically or physically, but feel unable to do anything about it.

The four types of psychological safety directly link into the four pillars of wellbeing. We cannot be happy if we are excluded. We cannot remain engaged if we feel we cannot contribute. Most importantly, we cannot stay safe and healthy if we feel unable to challenge something dangerous.

The danger of being psychologically unsafe

Psychological safety can be dismissed as a 'nice-to-have' with the emphasis remaining on physical safety. But you cannot have one without the other. You can never be truly safe in work without having the psychological safety to speak up. A lack of psychological safety has significant implications for physical safety and risk management.

We've all been there. Perhaps a colleague is giving a presentation and gesticulating enthusiastically, while all we are focused on is the very full glass of water right next to their laptop and their rapidly moving hands. Do we say anything? Hmmm … they are mid-flow and we don't want to interrupt them, or make them look careless, so no. But not speaking up leads to instant regret when we watch the water flood the laptop and the socket it's plugged into.

Risks aren't always small. Where there is very real risk of harm, possible risk to life, then we need to be able to speak, question and challenge freely. If we don't, then the consequences can be disastrous.

Meet Phil

There's one incident I've never forgotten. We had a young apprentice with us on the factory floor, and our supervisor was really odd and liked to intimidate the younger lads. It was really unpleasant and I tried to be extra nice to them to compensate. This poor lad joined us, and the supervisor just would not stop giving out to him. I felt so sorry for him, and at his workstation I saw him push his safety glasses up and wipe his eyes. I think he was emotional, and I wanted to give him a minute to compose himself so that I didn't embarrass him. He left the safety glasses on top of his head. I saw it but I didn't want to shout across the shop floor and draw attention to him, as I didn't want the supervisor having a go at him. Being completely honest, I didn't want that supervisor to have a go at me either. He was really off if we questioned anything or showed him up, and he could be really unpleasant. So, I left it. Next thing, this lad was screaming. He'd been leaning over a machine and some of the fluid had shot up and hit him square in the eye. Luckily, it was the cleaning oil and not the usual chemical mix that runs through that machine or he'd have been instantly blinded. As it was, the oil was hot and contaminated with some remaining chemicals. He had to go to hospital and have an emergency procedure as his eye and all around it was burned. He was in so much pain. He couldn't drive for months, which meant he couldn't work. Our supervisor was horrible about it and complained endlessly about the incident paperwork. He didn't realize he was the very reason I hadn't said anything and that this poor lad had moved his glasses in the first place. I wish I'd said something. I've never forgiven myself for that. He could have gone blind because I was too afraid of annoying someone else. That's a stupid reason to lose your eyesight.

Why we don't speak up

If you've been in Phil's position, or similar, where you saw something at work which you didn't challenge or question, but really wish you had, you are not alone. Seventy-four per cent of teams are not having psychological safety instilled in them by leaders,[4] and this is perpetuating an uncomfortable silence. Try to let go of any guilt around your silence.

Of course, we want to speak up if we see something we disagree with, or that makes us uncomfortable, but it isn't always easy. There are behaviours and cultures that diminish psychological safety and prevent us speaking up. We've touched on bias in hiring and promoting, and there can be linked inhibitors to our ability to speak up. We cannot be what we cannot see. If we don't see ourselves represented in wide-ranging and diverse teams that are role-modelling questioning, then we may feel inhibited to challenge or speak up.

Meet Amelia

I was the first Black woman to be a board member at the company I work for and although I felt very proud of that, I also felt inhibited and I didn't have great psychological safety at the beginning. I was very aware that I was not only the only person of colour but also the only woman. Sometimes I would raise an issue or challenge and I'd have their view explained back to me. It wasn't that I didn't understand, but that I didn't agree, but they weren't used to being challenged and it was hard to get my point across. It came to a head one day over the company's response to the Black Lives Matter movement. Everyone turned to face me, and I laughed awkwardly and said, 'Respectfully, it's not my attitude that needs to change!' This seemed to break the ice and got people talking, and we started to embrace more open discussion. It was definitely a turning point but it saddens me that I didn't feel listened to on earlier topics. One huge positive is that other people now challenge and question us as a board, because they have seen a real shift and change in the discussion, and I am proud of that. I did that. I only wish someone had done that for me. If I could go back, I'd push them harder because now I know they can have the challenge put to them, but at the time I hadn't seen it happen and wasn't confident in what the outcome of challenging them would be.

The behaviour of others is a huge influence on our ability to challenge, question and remain curious. If we feel belittled or are met with anger and defensiveness, then this is an extra barrier to achieving psychological safety. Some companies, even today, hold with a hierarchical system and really don't want people to challenge or question those above them. These antiquated ideas are usually the realm of those with fragile egos who see questions as threats. But knowing this doesn't make them any less intimidating to confront.

HHSE boost: Reflection

Pay attention to your psychological safety over the next week at work and reflect on the following:

- Do you feel safe at work?
- Can you challenge those around you to work differently?
- Are there any uncomfortable challenges that need overcoming?
- What is the impact on your own HHSE score?
- What would you like to be different to boost your psychological safety?

In her punchy TEDx talk, Professor Edmondson describes an inbuilt self-preservation mechanism known as 'impression management'.[5] This is the process by which we try to control the impressions others form of us, and it plays an important role in interpersonal behaviours.[6]

These techniques of self-preservation and impression management stem from childhood experiences. As children we want to be accepted into friendship groups and are discouraged from questioning or challenging others. Given they start at such an early age, these behaviours are extremely well established and habitual by the time we start work. Indeed, so much of this behaviour is second nature to us that we may not even realize we are doing it.

This is not good news for the workplace. For a workplace to thrive, it needs people who can challenge, question, explore, be curious and innovative, and who are prepared to try and fail. A seemingly counterintuitive finding is that higher-performing teams make a lot more mistakes. On examining the research further, we find that these teams actually have higher levels of psychological safety than lower-performing teams, which allows them to discuss, report and record mistakes.[7] It's not that they are making more mistakes than other teams, it is that they feel safe enough to admit to them.

Edmondson states that, without psychological safety, we experience anxiety and feel stuck in a place where we are uncomfortable with the situation, but equally feel uncomfortable to change or challenge it. This ultimately leads to disengagement. We can't be happy, healthy, safe and engaged if we are psychologically unsafe at work.

Fear of failure is challenging enough in itself, as we battle our own inner critic and imposter syndrome, but it's ten times worse if we fear something bad will happen as a result of speaking up.

Why do we always fear the worst?

Our brain will always fear the worst and present a worst-case scenario. If you get an email from your boss out of the blue saying, 'We need to talk, can we meet at 4 p.m. today?', your brain won't spend the rest of the day planning how to spend your imminent pay rise. Instead, it will worry and replay conversations and maybe even plan a defence of your role, because your brain assumes you are about to be fired. This is not your brain trying to be difficult. Quite the opposite in fact: your brain thinks it's being helpful. The brain's main purpose is to keep us alive and that means it will constantly scan for threat. Therefore, an unprompted and vague email kicks our brain into panicked overdrive and we begin to worry, even if it then transpires that your boss just wanted to confirm the date of a conference you mentioned. Phew!

Often, we get cross with ourselves for being paranoid or stressing out too much about work, but it isn't our fault. There are many reasons why our brain can be particularly hypervigilant around threat in the workplace.

A history of insecurity

Dysfunctional families have a lot to answer for, as they continue to impact our growth and development and how we challenge ourselves well into adulthood. If you grew up unable to question or challenge situations in the home, then you didn't develop the skillset to do so in the workplace.

It's not a blame game, but rather a process of identifying where we might need to do the work. By recognizing that we may not have the skillset, then we know where we need to put our energy and focus to support ourselves. Remember the power of neuroplasticity? It doesn't matter if we don't know how to do something; we can learn how to do it. But we don't know what we don't know. This again is why quitting won't solve anything. If we don't have a skillset or confidence in one job, we won't magically gain it in another job. We have to do the work and build our skills.

Redundant feelings

Redundancies are a trauma for a company. They cause disruptions, split teams, change dynamics and adjust workloads for those remaining. They also have a huge impact on the psychological safety of those left behind. Redundancies cause fear in those remaining in role, and they feel guilt for surviving the cut, but they also feel angry about the future.

I often get drafted in to support companies through redundancies and it is a tense and emotional time for all employees, whether their roles are put at risk or not. In the very best-case scenarios, all redundancies are voluntary and the people who leave want to do so. However, for many this isn't the case, and regardless the outcome is a shift in team dynamics.

It can be hard for those remaining in employment to garner sympathy but it is incredibly challenging to be left behind. Those who remain often face a double-edged sword as not only do they have to deliver the bad news and face the emotion and challenges that come with that, but they are often the same people tasked with motivating the remaining workforce and rebuilding the company. This is even more challenging when we consider the research that suggests redundancies rarely achieve the desired aim and so those involved are likely to strongly disagree with, yet have to be complicit in, seeing it through.[8]

Screaming into a void

Companies often cite 'survey fatigue' as a problem. However, very few of us are going to be fatigued by completing a few questionnaires. We don't have survey fatigue; we are sick of screaming into a void.

While leaders see the background work generated by an employee engagement survey, the rest of us complete the survey and … nothing happens. We don't see the management committees and task groups set up in order to tackle the issues raised, especially in a larger company. Often the results of a survey may take three to six months to filter back to every employee, if indeed they do at all.

This means, from an employee perspective, we speak up, offer our opinion, and put time and energy into completing the survey, but then nothing happens. We are fatigued by the lack of response, not the survey. Moreover, we don't just wait until the annual survey comes around in order to share our opinions. We will have been airing our suggestions and potential grievances to our managers and peers for some time, which can make being issued an employee survey particularly grating. We have already shared our opinions and they have been ignored, so why would we now put them in writing?

We all have that friend who constantly asks for advice but never takes it. Instead, every phone call is a circular conversation coming back to their same situation and how they are feeling about it. No matter what you suggest, it is ignored. Next time they ring you, how enthusiastic are you feeling about taking their call? This is how we feel about completing yet another survey. We don't have telephone fatigue and we don't have survey fatigue; we are all simply fed up of not being listened to.[9]

All three of these experiences explain why our brain is prone to expect the worst and it's important that we recognize these impacts so that we can start to overcome them and build our own sense of safety. These scenarios may be familiar to us but there are other, newer ideas around psychological safety, or a lack of it, affecting us at work. One of these is 'leavism'.

Leavism

You've probably experienced absenteeism when you've been off work due to sickness, and you are likely to have been one of the 80 per cent of us who experiences presenteeism (where we are at work in body but not spirit). Presenteeism means we clock up our hours but are not being productive.

This happens for myriad reasons ranging from sickness through to demotivation.

Leavism is a fairly new concept, first outlined in a 2014 study. This is the practice where we will take annual leave, or paid time off, in order to catch up on our work. We are feeling an increased pressure to work when away on annual leave, with more of us than ever before checking emails or completing projects during the time we should be relaxing and unwinding.

There is also a trend of not using sick leave, even if paid sickness absence is available, and instead using annual leave to recover from illness. Leavism suggests that the most basic level of psychological safety, inclusion safety, is not available to us. Now, some people have their own reasons for choosing to work while on holiday. For many, feeling as though they are necessary and need to be available to work can be the result of anxiety, or may even provide an all-important ego boost. It is very flattering and inflating if we believe the company will fall apart without us (even if it isn't actually true).

However, those of us who feel it is not a choice and as though we have to take annual leave in order to catch up with work are on our way to burnout. It is important to pay attention to the lack of psychological safety that may be driving this behaviour.

The modern workplace is crowded and noisy. A constant stream of chatter and noise from Slack, Yammer, Teams, Zoom, Skype and Outlook means we are surrounded daily by a cacophony of noise and interruptions. I myself have threatened on many occasions to throw my laptop out of the window simply to give myself a break (thankfully I realized I could just switch off notifications before that expensive incident occurred). This may lead us to feel as though we need a week where we can be left alone, without interruption, in order to crack on with tasks and catch up with ourselves. Even typing that I can feel the pressure release at the thought of uninterrupted time purely to focus on clearing a few tasks without more pouring in at the top. However, with inclusion safety, we know that we can simply ask for this. We can say to our boss, 'Hey, I'm a bit overwhelmed and I need to take some time to catch up.' Without inclusion safety, we feel the need to hide this part of us and use our leave, evenings and weekends, as though we will be chastised or somehow thought less of.

The challenge here is that it's not a failing to not be able to keep up with an unreasonable workload. It's human. With inclusion safety we'd feel comfortable to show this side of ourselves and know that we are still in the gang, but without it we feel as though we need to hide it. This can be the start of imposter syndrome, where we fear being caught out – an issue we will talk about later.

Meet Shona

As a manager, if an employee comes to me and asks if they can take some uninterrupted time and miss a few meetings in order to crack on with work, then I am delighted. I am always impressed when someone can assess their needs and take proactive steps to prevent future problems. If an employee needs to catch up, but does nothing about it and doesn't discuss it with me, then they will continue to fall behind and feel increased stress and pressure and I'll be none the wiser. This is why I think we all have to prioritize and take care of our own psychological safety. Your manager cannot be aware of how you are feeling, and all the pressures you are under within work, all the time, as much of it won't be visible to them. It is only through having clear and transparent conversations that your manager can support you. I really value those conversations with my team. They really make me feel trusted, and I get an opportunity to help and support, which is my job as a manager after all!

Building your safety

If we are struggling in a role, or feeling demotivated, then putting in the work to change it may not be appealing. But remember, this isn't about working for your role. This is about doing the work for you. About being the happiest and healthiest version of you that you can be. Gaining psychological safety, developing the confidence to speak up when something doesn't feel right, or clashes with your values, is a skill for life. Work is a safe space to practise and hone those skills.

We need to challenge our brain's natural worst-case scenario tendency, which tells us challenging something will be a disaster and lead to conflict. It is not unreasonable to ask for help and support at work, and it is important to know that our brain is just trying to protect us, but that doesn't make those worst-case thoughts *facts*.

I have worked with many individuals who falsely predict their manager's or teammate's response to a request by mind-reading what others will think of them, and then the reality is nothing like they imagined.

Meet Donna

I'd wanted to change my hours and condense my week for a while. I really struggled with how I'd be perceived, and whether people would think I was slacking. Many people around me worked the sort of hours I was suggesting, but they did those five days per week. I was asking to do it for four. I put the idea to my manager in a really stumbling and caveat-filled way. I'd convinced myself that she would think badly of me, call me lazy, and even tell me that, if I didn't want to work hard, then she'd find someone else who would! I wasn't confident at all, but I also knew that my current working week wasn't sustainable. She didn't even blink. She just said, 'OK, that makes sense. We need sign-off from the director so I'll start the paperwork and send it on.' I was gobsmacked. I had prepared myself for battle, and she didn't even question me or challenge the idea at all. I had bottled out of the conversation so many times and within two months was working my condensed week. Imagine if I'd asked six months before, I would have been so much healthier as a result. I had been my own blocker. I had imagined so many conversations and arguments and consequences, and none of them came true.

Donna had trapped herself into believing no psychological safety existed, whereas her manager was very happy to have the conversation and support her suggestion.

HHSE boost: Reflection

- Have you been avoiding a situation at work because you've been fearing the worst or mind-reading someone else's response?

- How can you challenge this belief?
- What can you explore over the coming week that could cause a positive change for you at work?

There is a lot of emphasis on leaders doing more to ensure psychological safety in their teams, and there is no doubt that there is a role for leaders to play in building a trusting environment where it is safe to fail. But it isn't only down to them. Often, we create our own diminishers for psychological safety. We question ourselves, doubt ourselves, experience peaks of anxiety which automatically freeze us, meaning we don't ask, question or challenge.

We need to work on our own self-stigmas and beliefs and become mindful of which behaviours support our development, learning and curiosity, and of which behaviours keep us anxious. We have to build our own locus of control and not rely on others to make us feel safe about speaking up. We must trust ourselves to build and grow the confidence, which quickly transforms into psychological safety for those around us.

We develop these unhelpful habits of trying to fit in and not question the status quo, not 'rocking the boat', so early on and then carry these habits into the workplace. Remember the basic 'do no harm' principle, where you don't harm work and work doesn't harm you? Well, this is one way you may be harming your workplace. When you silence yourself, you prevent growth and engagement. Your idea, question or challenge could be the difference between a mediocre 'that's how we've always done it' approach and an award-winning pitch. When we limit ourselves to just turning up, we are arriving disengaged.

The engagement piece often throws people. It takes them back to their youth and wanting to appear too cool for school, not a keen bean at the front of the class with their hand up. We almost get embarrassed by being good at our job, by wanting to engage in our work, being enthusiastic or wanting to better something. Here's the thing. You're not at school anymore. You need to shrug off your teenage embarrassment and step into your adult workplace self – not to please your boss but for your own health, happiness and psychological safety. You have so much potential and energy within you, and engaging in your work, through questioning, learning and trying, will lead you to experience higher HHSE every single day. Psychological safety is a key skill, and you can start building it today. Look around you at work for something you can try, change or learn from. What can you make better? What can you link to your values? What can you notice that you have previously walked by?

Reworking psychological safety

- We cannot have safety without psychological safety.
- It is dangerous to be in a situation where we cannot speak up.
- It's not about being 'brave' – there are many past influencing factors which affect our ability to speak up.
- We can challenge and overcome our tendency to expect the worst. Things are never as bad as we fear, but we only learn that through taking action and doing.
- Work is a brilliant place to grow our psychological safety skills, as it has a knock-on wider impact and will serve us in all areas of our lives.

6

Stress

Stress. Even the word can be enough to get our blood pressure rising. It seemed near impossible to write a book about workplace wellbeing and not include a chapter or two on stress. Stress is the co-worker we never asked for but seem stuck with. It accompanies us to meetings, loiters in our inbox, and even follows us home and invites itself to dinner. Sometimes stress slips into bed with us, stealing sleep and making us restless. No matter how unwelcome stress is, it seems we cannot avoid it in the modern workplace.

We will look at why life is so stressful and what we are dealing with in the workplace a little later, but first I want to tell you about your stress response. I passionately believe that we should all know how our brain works. Once we understand what is happening in our brains and bodies, then our responses are demystified and we understand why we feel the way we do. Once we understand the why within our bodies, we can understand why situations affect us in the way that they do, and we can decide what does and doesn't work for us.

So many people think stress is all in their mind. They tell me that they should just be able to 'get a grip' and not stress out so much, as though they have control over what is essentially an ancient biological process. If you've ever cried in the car on your way to work, slammed down your coffee mug, snapped at your children, or felt as though you are going ever so slightly mad, then you can probably thank your stress response. I have been in jobs so stressful that cognitively I felt fine, yet sat shaking on an underground railway train, praying for a drivers' strike (they never happen when you need them!) so that I wouldn't have to face another day in the office. I told myself I was pathetic. I told myself to get a grip. I told myself to be grateful. What I forgot to do was calm my body.

Our stress response is powerful and floods us with many physical and emotional symptoms, sometimes catching us unawares and leading us to feel wrongfooted and even frightened. It isn't a personality trait or weakness to get stressed. It is a natural response to external stimuli. But we don't need to be disadvantaged by it. Once we understand our stress response and exactly what activates it and how it works, we can mitigate negative impacts and even use our stress response to our advantage.

This chapter is dedicated to the science of your stress response. This is essential learning to stop blaming ourselves for feeling anxious or overwhelmed or any other by-product of stress. Our response to stress is a simple matter of connections and processes in the brain, all of which happen automatically and without conscious input. We shouldn't fear our stress response, we should harness it.

Reflection: How do you know when you are stressed?

Take a moment to think about your own response to stress.

- How do you know when you are stressed?
- What do you notice in your body?
- How is your mood?

- How are your sleep and appetite?
- What do other people notice about you?
- If I saw you walking towards me on the street, how would I know that you were stressed?
- How does stress help, or hinder, you day-to-day?

Reflecting on the above questions, take a moment to recognize what the impact of stressful events is on your mind and body. Know that whatever you notice is normal. Our stress response, as we will see, affects us in myriad ways, and there is no such thing as a 'wrong' response to stress, even if some of it feels unhelpful. Your stress response is your body doing what it is supposed to do, and we will learn how to use this response to help us, in whatever we are trying to achieve or get through. Your stress response is about to become your superpower.

Stress response – the basics

It all starts with the amygdala. The amygdala is the alarm bell of the brain. Whenever our amygdala perceives danger or threat, it sounds the alarm and alerts the hypothalamus. Your hypothalamus acts as a command centre and communicates with the rest of your body through your autonomic nervous system. For example, if your amygdala detects threat, the hypothalamus connects to your adrenal glands which start flooding your body with adrenaline. Adrenaline is powerful stuff and causes immediate physiological changes. Racing heart? Adrenaline. Feeling shaky? Adrenaline. Breathing more rapidly? Adrenaline.

You won't be aware of the process at all, only the resulting sensations and changes. When something happens, your reaction will be instantaneous. This incredible response means we can have immediate and life-saving reactions. But it doesn't stop there.

That autonomic nervous system has two components: your *sympathetic* (not as nice as it sounds) and your *parasympathetic* systems. Think of them as the child (sympathetic) and the parent (parasympathetic). When the alarm bell rings it is your sympathetic nervous system that responds. This excitable child starts jumping up and down and overreacting and generally causing chaos. It is your parasympathetic nervous system (PNS) that then has to step in and be the parent, calming down and balancing the sympathetic nervous system response. One analogy has it that the sympathetic nervous system screams, 'There's a snake in the road!' while your parasympathetic nervous system responds, 'Calm down – it's just a piece of rope.'

It is our sympathetic nervous system that triggers a fight-or-flight response when we are stressed. If a lion walks into the room, your amygdala is going to sound the alarm. Your sympathetic nervous system is going to respond and give you a burst of energy to get you out of danger. This means your heart pounds, pushing blood to your muscles and vital organs. Your breathing changes, sending extra oxygen to your brain to increase alertness. Your senses such as sight and hearing become sharper. Also, sugar (glucose) and fat are released into your bloodstream to supply energy to all parts of the body.

This beautifully orchestrated process happens in a millisecond and ultimately saves us from the lion. There are a few kinks in the system, though. One, we don't have many lions walking into meeting rooms and so our natural stress response can feel very over the top for the workplace. Two, our brain cannot tell the difference between actual threat and imagined threat. This means we can activate our stress response simply by thinking about something that might (but probably won't) happen in the future, or by recalling an uncomfortable memory. Humans are the experts in overthinking, living in the past or worrying about the future, and we rarely stay in the present moment, which results in a fairly constant activation of our stress response. Three, our amygdala is not consistent.

Pumping up the volume!

Our amygdala works like a volume switch. If we are feeling pretty good and safe and are in good health overall, then our amygdala starts at a low volume and everything is responded to in a rational and calm way. However, there are factors which turn our amygdala volume up, ranging from a poor night's sleep through to unpleasant events or traumas in our past. These and many other factors mean that our amygdala is getting louder and louder, and this makes our reactions and stress response more extreme. You'll know when your amygdala is turned up. On a quiet-volume day someone cuts you up in traffic and you think, 'Oof, I hope they get there safely.' On a loud-amygdala day? You're honking the horn and gifting them with some choice language and hand gestures. Same situation, different volume. These are the days when tangled earphones or a broken zip will have you enraged. These are also the days when you are less pleasant to be around.

At work, there may be many minor stresses that slowly crank up the volume, ever so gently so that we don't really notice how stressed we are until an email lands or a project deadline moves and we feel overwhelmed. We are flooded with physical symptoms of stress, leaving us feeling physically and emotionally awful.

Let's review and understand some of the common symptoms of stress, caused by our sympathetic nervous system reactions.

Headache

Our pupils dilate to allow us to take in a lot of visual information, handy when we need to spot the exit and quickly escape from that lion. But when sitting at our laptop, if our pupils dilate, then suddenly lights are too bright and we feel headachy. Also, with our heightened senses and alertness, noises can be too loud. A classic example of this is when we reach a tricky junction and have to turn our car radio down so we can concentrate. The music level hasn't changed, but our response to it has. Heightened senses are great for outrunning that lion, but the same cannot be said for our workplace. Nothing changes externally but, when stressed, we are unable to block out the noise of others working, we cannot concentrate. Everything suddenly feels too much, too bright, too loud, too noisy. No wonder we get a headache.

Dry mouth

Have you ever felt the need to cough or clear your throat when you're stressed? I call this the stress cough, and if you haven't noticed this irritating, persistent cough, then those around you probably will have! Our saliva is inhibited because when we experience fight or flight, our body isn't interested in breaking down food. But if we are trying to give a presentation or have a challenging conversation, then having a very dry mouth and throat can be deeply unpleasant. This is why we often need a glass of water when stressed or nervous.

Racing heart

All the adrenaline coursing through our body can raise our heart rate, and when we aren't expecting it, a racing heart can feel very scary. If you are trying to relax in the evening, but you are still thinking about work or processing your working day, then you can be quietly watching a film and your heart starts pounding. We may even worry that there is something seriously wrong with our heart, which in turn causes more fear and more adrenaline, and more symptoms.

Stomach ache

Our sympathetic nervous system has an impact on peristalsis, which is the muscular movement through our digestive tract. Put crudely, this means that when we are stressed, either nothing moves (constipation) or everything moves (diarrhoea). This is why when we are stressed, we are so prone to symptoms of irritable bowel syndrome such as bloating and feeling uncomfortable. These issues also cause changes in appetite where we either eat nothing at all because we feel nauseated or we overeat. Comfort eating is so called because it works. When we are struggling to digest food properly the high fat and sugary foods we crave offer some much needed feel-good for the brain. Unfortunately, the effects don't last and can often compound digestive issues we are having. So many of us lose control over food when we are stressed, but we shouldn't be hard on ourselves. This reaction is driven by our stress response, and it's only by understanding and changing that response that we can expect behavioural change. Being cross with yourself for stress eating, or not eating well enough, is a bit like being kicked in the leg all day and then being cross with yourself for needing crutches. Your body is doing its best and asking for what it needs. Be kind to yourself in these moments. You will be much more in control once you understand and recognize the triggers leading you to this point.

Bladder impacts

When stressed, your bladder contractions and voiding are impacted, which explains why you may need the toilet a lot more frequently, but not feel as though your bladder empties. When stressed, you don't have the same control and contraction as you have when you feel relaxed. This can lead to increased worry about getting to or being near a toilet, which is not always easy at work. With the sensations being increased along with our stress levels, often even a tiny amount of urine can be interpreted as a full bladder, and with that increased urgency and discomfort can be experienced.

Getting fatter

It's not just the comfort eating that makes us pile on the pounds when we are stressed. All that glucose and fat being released into our system is there to fuel us for running or movement. If we are sitting still at our desk or work bench and don't burn it off, then all that glucose and fat gets reabsorbed, meaning stress can make us fatter.

Exhaustion

Do you struggle to move more when stressed? Are you overcome with fatigue, making even a short walk or climbing the stairs exhausting? Again, this is due to the messages in your brain getting louder. You may not actually be any more tired or exhausted than you are normally, but your brain is much more aware of your tiredness. This often clashes with a more fidgety side of us that struggles to sit still when experiencing stress. This restless feeling is caused by the adrenaline and a primitive urge to run. Again, this is very useful if you are running from a lion, but less useful when stuck in a meeting room for three hours. This can leave us caught between the urge to move but feeling too exhausted to do so.

Longer term, living in a permanently stressed-out state is exhausting for your mind and body, and our bodies are clever. If we don't stop and look after ourselves, our bodies will break down somewhere and make us stop, even if that is stopping us getting out of bed. This is where tiredness is your body trying to drop you a not so subtle hint: 'Stop and look after me or I will force you to stop.' But feeling very tired and stressed leads us to feel overwhelmed. Remember, though, it will be OK – this is just our bodies responding naturally to the stimuli of stress. Although unpleasant, it's what is supposed to happen.

I'm so stressed, I can't even think straight

There is one other very common side effect to being stressed that is less talked about but which negatively impacts us both at home and at work and it is worth knowing about. This is the inability to think straight or make decisions when we are stressed.

If you are under huge pressure or stress, you may find that your decision-making ability goes out of the window. Someone asks you if you want tea or coffee and you freeze. Your partner asks you what you want for dinner, and the decision somehow feels momentous and overwhelming. You may find these are the moments when you are snappy or sharp with other people, because you cannot think straight. It all feels too much. These are also the days when you cannot stop thinking about work, but don't actually get much done. What on earth is happening in your brain to give you such a sense of confusion, brain fog and congestion in your train of thought?

Again, it starts with your amygdala, but this time we want to also think of the hippocampus (your office manager) and your prefrontal cortex (your CEO). Your hippocampus works incredibly hard. It is responsible for the filing and sorting of your brain and is involved in learning and memory tasks. The prefrontal cortex is responsible for the rational, thinking, planning part of you. This CEO part of the brain often relies on the hippocampus to remember previous incidents, which can then override some of the amygdala's overexcited tendencies, before strong fight-or-flight reactions are triggered.

As you go through your day learning, absorbing and processing information, then your hippocampus is methodically working away, filing and sorting all this information for you. We don't often realize that all information we absorb has to be processed. There is no way to say to our brain, 'Don't bother with this one, it doesn't matter.' Everything has to be filed and sorted by the hippocampus, from important legal documents through to the videos and reels you casually scroll through while waiting in a queue.

When we are stressed, the function of the hippocampus is impacted and becomes overwhelmed and struggles to support the prefrontal cortex to make decisions. This means that someone asks us a straightforward question and we cannot process and retrieve the information to provide an answer.

When stressed, we stop thinking clearly and we experience something called *amygdala hijack*. Once again, our amygdala is at the forefront, and amygdala hijack is what happens when the reactions of the amygdala are not tempered by the rational thinking prefrontal cortex or the experience and learning of the hippocampus. The amygdala goes rogue and throws us into fight-or-flight mode at the drop of a hat, meaning even simple tasks can feel overwhelming and cause a strong reaction. We may get a fairly innocuous email and throw the laptop on the floor, or type a two-word reply ending in 'off'. These are not good, rational and well-thought-out responses, and they can land us in real difficulty.

It's also why it's not a good idea to make important decisions when stressed, and why we are prone to more risk-taking behaviours. In a safety-critical environment, amygdala hijack can be fatal. Your amygdala doesn't care about future you; it only wants to feel good now. In *this* moment. If you accidentally dropped a tool in the middle of a working machine, your experienced hippocampus and prefrontal cortex would tell you to turn the machine off, wait until everything has cooled down, and then use the appropriate tool to retrieve what you have dropped. Your amygdala would tell you to just reach in and grab it – yikes! We see people engage in what appears to be stupid and reckless behaviour, but they may not be making that choice – their amygdala may be choosing for them.

This now-me versus future-me battle is also why the amygdala can sabotage your goals. You may have great intentions of going to the gym after work, but your amygdala decides that it'd rather stay on the sofa and eat ice cream. If the amygdala has taken over, then that's what you will do because you are in the throes of amygdala hijack.

These are just some of the impacts of our stress response, and don't account for the sensations or emotions we feel with prolonged activation. We can see there is a strong physiological and emotional impact of our stress response, but what about the calming parent I mentioned previously? Where is the parasympathetic nervous system that we need to calm us down?

Here's the kicker. When we are stressed, our parasympathetic nervous system gets dampened. This is to allow our sympathetic nervous system to do its thing and get us ready to escape a lion (after all, now is not the time to hear 'I'm sure it'll be fine – it's just a giant kitten'). When we need our parasympathetic nervous system the most, we have the least access to it.

But all is not lost. We can take steps to mitigate these responses, calm our amygdala down, activate our parasympathetic nervous system and generally rein in our stress response so that it becomes a measured and helpful reaction. We can then use our stress response to our advantage.

When we get to know our stress response then we are no longer passengers but drivers. We cannot control everything, nor should we want to – our brains are far cleverer and more capable of handling our response to stress and threat than we are. If it was a conscious cognitive process, we'd probably all be dead, as our instantaneous response is what keeps us safe from harm. However, when we are at work, we don't need such extreme responses and we don't need to feel anything like as awful as we do. After all, feeling this way can't be good for you. Can it?

Is stress damaging me?

Your stress response is your body doing exactly what it is supposed to do. In recent years, we have been confronted with headlines saying that stress is as bad for us as smoking and describing stress as a 'silent killer'. While the physical experience of your stress response can feel deeply unpleasant, it isn't *dangerous*. Your stress response is exactly that – a response. We have been taught to fear stress, but these symptoms are actually signs of your body handling stress like a boss. You are prepared, you are fuelled, you are ready.

In her amazing TED Talk health psychologist Kelly McGonigal talks about the power of changing our reaction to stress. Ironically, our normal and typical stress response won't cause us any harm, but worrying about our normal and typical stress response *can* cause us harm. If we can accept our stress response as the correct response to a threat, then we physiologically respond to stress differently. If you feel your heart pounding and your senses heightening and can say to yourself, 'My body is rising to this challenge and I will respond exactly how I am supposed to', then research shows that our cardiovascular reaction shifts and we remain in a state of preparedness but without the negative impacts.

Our stress response isn't the problem. Our problem is believing that a perfectly natural response in our brains and bodies is damaging us. It isn't. Yes, prolonged and unnecessary activation of your stress response takes its toll. But the actual stress response itself is your body doing what it is supposed to do and we have to have faith in our brains and bodies. They know what they are doing. Our brains even support us with healing hormones such as oxytocin to mop up after any damage caused by an initial stress response, and our parasympathetic nervous system comes into play to soothe and calm us. Our brains know what they are doing, even if we don't. Our role is to mitigate and minimize the risks that are causing a constant and unnecessary activation of our stress response, which includes turning the volume of our amygdala down and supporting our body so that it can perform at its best through stressful times.

When we support our bodies through stress, we are able to use our stress response to our advantage. We get all the benefits of being alert, ready and fuelled, and experience a massive reduction of the more unpleasant side effects. It's important that we recognize the aim here is not to eliminate our stress response. This response is well honed and beautiful, and we need it. It protects us. But we can support and enhance that protection and use stress as an ally.

Harnessing your stress response

There are ways of using your stress response to your advantage, and these involve some simple reframing in our minds. Simply changing the way we view stress, and our response to it, means that we will change our physiological experience of stress.

Try this neat trick. Your brain doesn't know the difference between being nervous and being excited, and both will elicit different responses in your brain. Next time you have a job interview or are in a situation that is making you feel nervous, tell yourself you are excited. Your brain will believe you and respond positively to support and enhance your experience. Even if you are truly nervous, telling yourself that you are excited will settle your stomach and bladder, leaving you feeling energized and prepared for whatever lies ahead. You may even begin to look forward to the event or situation that previously had you feeling nervously stressed.

Activating your parasympathetic nervous system

Although, with its calming and soothing properties, parasympathetic activity sounds lovely, we wouldn't be able to solely have parasympathetic activity because then we'd have no motivation. We'd never get out of bed, and we'd just float about not achieving much. This might sound heavenly for a few hours, but, in reality, we need the oomph of the sympathetic nervous system. It gets us going, helps us to achieve and keeps us active. But neither can we live solely in sympathetic mode because we would be in a shaky, adrenaline-fuelled state, unable to eat or sleep properly, and constantly having toilet issues. We need balance. Ideally, our bodies would like to have a 50/50 balance so we have a good blend of rest and digest and movement and motivation.

As mentioned before, when we are stressed, it is our sympathetic nervous system that is activated and our parasympathetic nervous system that is dampened. In order to readdress the balance and feel better when stressed, we need to deliberately activate our parasympathetic nervous system. This will calm down our physical response and allow us to feel much better and at ease in our bodies. Changing our approach to work will contribute to a healthier and more balanced stress response. However, there are some very specific techniques to immediately activate your parasympathetic nervous system, three of which are summarized below.

Take a nice deep breath? I don't think so

Have you ever been really stressed and some helpful person has told you to take a nice deep breath? That's terrible advice. Much like with asthma, when we are stressed, it isn't the inhale that is the problem, it is the exhale. We are full of stale air as we shallow breathe and sip air through hyperventilation. If you say to someone who is stressed, 'Take a nice deep breath', most likely they won't be able to, and so all you have done there is make them worry that they aren't breathing properly! Instead of focusing on the inhale, focus on the exhale. Breathe in however you can and then exhale noisily, blowing your cheeks out, like a child blowing out birthday candles. Now, you have expelled a lot of stale air and made room for fresh air to come in. Now you can take that deep inhale that was being pushed on you before, and then continue breathing while focusing on your exhale. If your exhale is longer than your inhale, then you are activating your parasympathetic nervous system. You don't need to keep exhaling strongly after that first big blow out. In fact, you don't need the dramatic sigh at all, I just like the stress-busting nature of a good huff.

If you keep breathing normally, but make your exhale a little longer than your inhale every time, it will work. This will have a calming effect on your body and start to release the grip of your stress response. This is a great tool to use if ever you are lying awake at night, tired but too wired to sleep. This gentle activation of your parasympathetic nervous system will ease you into a sleepier state.

You can use this technique anywhere, at your desk, on the train, behind your workbench. Wherever you are, you always have your breath, so use it to your advantage.

Yoga

I know, I know. Believe me I know. If you are feeling stressed and wound up, the thought of being still and sitting on a yoga mat can be less than appealing. However, yoga is proven to activate the parasympathetic nervous system. In fact, the benefits of breath–body movement go beyond the parasympathetic and actually cause changes in the brain. Yoga has been shown to reshape the hippocampus, allowing for information to be processed more freely. There is a neurological reason why people feel better after yoga. They are calmer, they think more clearly, they sleep better and they have better memories. Yoga rebalances the autonomic nervous system, and it doesn't need to be a long and complicated practice. There's no need for leggings or headstands here. The benefit comes from synchronized breath–body movement, so actually the best poses are going to be gentle, restorative and simple. Moving your body with intentional breath will mitigate your stress response, and a regular practice can reduce anxiety and depression. Start slowly, start gently, start where you are. Just start. Your body will thank you.

Being among nature

Being in nature activates our parasympathetic nervous system. Sitting or gently walking around in woods, forests or green spaces slows our heart rate and begins to gently repair any stress-related impacts on our bodies. Even a ten-minute walk around the neighbourhood can reduce your cortisol (stress hormone) levels significantly. If you cannot actually get out in nature, then bringing nature inside can also make a huge difference, either through house plants or being able to touch natural materials such as wood, leaves or feathers. If you are really stuck indoors, then research shows even time spent looking at pictures of nature is good for our parasympathetic nervous system.

These are some quick hacks for immediate parasympathetic nervous system activation, but there are many more ways to stimulate and balance your autonomic nervous system. The techniques outlined throughout this book will support your approach to a better-balanced work life and lead you to feel happier, healthier, safer and more engaged.

The next chapter looks at why stress is so prevalent in our working lives and what we can do to reduce the unnecessary yet constant activation of our stress response.

If nothing else, I hope this chapter, and the next, stop you blaming yourself for being stressed. We are supposed to feel stress. It's not a weakness, a character failing or a sign that we are not coping. It is our bodies responding to stressful stimuli, and it's what is supposed to happen.

When we embrace our stress response, we can harness it, using that energy, focus and drive to our advantage. Don't beat yourself up for feeling the way that you do. You're stressed enough already.

Reworking the stress response

- Our stress response is a well-honed and protective response, designed to get us out of harm's way quickly.

- It is not a character flaw to experience stress.

- Although wonderfully orchestrated, our stress response can be over the top for the modern workplace.

- Although uncomfortable to experience, our stress response is not damaging us, *but* prolonged and unnecessary activation is exhausting and unhealthy, so we want to mitigate the impacts where we can.

- Regular and deliberate parasympathetic nervous system activation will balance out our nervous system and make us feel more relaxed day-to-day.

7

Are You Stressed Yet?

The term used to be 'busy'. People would ask how work was going and you would say 'busy'. Busy equated to good. If you were busy in your store, it meant you had customers. If you were busy on the trading floor, then it meant you were making great commission. If you were busy in your factory, it meant you had many orders. If you had a busy social life, then you were considered popular and in demand by others. Busy became desirable and aspirational.

Alongside this definition of busy, we started to *expect* busyness. The harder we worked, the busier we became. If we were not busy, then we were deemed to not be working hard enough. If you had spare time in your day, then that was time that could, and should, be used. We began to view time as transactional, a means of getting tasks completed and items ticked off our to-do list. We emulated busy, and even if we weren't busy, we wanted to appear busy.

Imagine your boss walking by your workstation and asking, 'How are you getting on?' Would you be comfortable answering, 'I'm super relaxed. I don't have a lot on my plate right now. If anything, I'm almost a little bored'? Probably not. We expect busy, we chase busy, we reward busy.

Nowadays, the term more commonly used is stressed and stressed has become synonymous with busy, with both terms used interchangeably. We've transferred some of our old admiration and need for busy over to stressed. Indeed, some people wear their stress as a badge of honour, believing it makes them look more important, and busier, than the rest of us. We almost *need* to be stressed in order to feel successful. But have we lost sight of what stressed means?

The stress test

The physics definition describes stress as pressure or tension exerted on a material object. This is a great definition for how humans experience stress as well. We can actually tolerate a great deal of stress. Much like laying a pencil flat on the ground and standing on it with your entire body weight, you are unlikely to break it as the pressure is evenly distributed. However, if you hold each end and exert pressure in the centre, you can easily snap a pencil. This is how stress feels. If we have too many pressures unevenly distributed, in one or two areas of our lives, then we feel as though we are about to break.

The way we describe stress colloquially supports this definition. 'They are obviously *under* a lot of stress' is a phrase which conjures up the image of someone being underneath a heavy weight and facing up to a mountain of problems, pressures and challenges.

While we know that our stress response itself isn't damaging, there are consequences to chasing and maintaining stress.

The impact of stress on work

While we seem to accept a level of necessary stress within the workplace, prolonged and unhelpful stress has negative impacts. We see a reduction in engagement, productivity and job performance, as well as terse relationships with co-workers.[1]

Furthermore, high employee turnover, increased absenteeism and long working hours with reduced efficacy have also been attributed to stress within the workplace.

We ourselves recognize that we don't do a good job when stressed, with 91 per cent of us stating that feeling overwhelmingly stressed negatively affects the quality of our work.[2]

What does stress at work look like?

It isn't what we think. When we think of stress, we may picture steam coming out of our ears and thumping the desk, but, in reality, we are unlikely to see overtly stressed behaviour in the workplace. After all, it isn't socially acceptable to punch a wall, or our colleagues, and so stress at work looks very different from how we imagine.

At our most stressed, we may be that colleague who has withdrawn. The one who is sitting quietly in the corner, eyes down, head down, trying to get on with their work. Perhaps a little less sociable and chatty than usual, but definitely not the one screaming 'I'm so stressed!'.

We all have that one colleague who spends their time telling everyone how stressed they are. (You can't help but think that if they spent the time telling us all how stressed they are doing their work, then they wouldn't be nearly so stressed in the first place!) That colleague who is shouting and yelling and telling everyone that they are super stressed is at least finding an outlet and a channel for their stress ... but what about their more quiet and introverted colleagues? Where is their outlet? This has implications for both finding and seeking help for stress at work. People may think, 'Of course I'd help and support my colleague if they were overwhelmed,' but the truth is they may not know how stressed you are. In a world where hybrid and flexible working are increasingly the norm, and the most face-to-face interaction we have with people is through a small square on a screen, this can be even harder to spot and identify.

Changes in working practice have allowed us to become more skilled at faking it and hiding our stress. We can all put a smile on our faces for an hour or pretend our camera is broken in order to avoid showing our true emotions. The stress hasn't gone anywhere; it's just less visible.

Conversely, even though we accept and anticipate stress more now than in previous generations, many of us hold an internal bias against stress. While we use the term 'stressed' freely, we don't want to be labelled as 'stressed', with nearly half of us believing that admitting to stress could prevent getting a promotion or pay rise. The fear stems from associating stress with not coping and seeing it as a flaw in our system. When stress at work is so often well hidden, it is easy to assume that everyone else is absolutely fine while we feel as though we are falling apart like wet cake. We assume that there must be something wrong with us and our way of coping if we are continually feeling more stressed than others seem.

So many individuals I support start by telling me they are stressed to the skull, and how they feel they should just be coping better. However, our current stress levels are not our fault. We are living in a perfect storm of stress-triggering events, combined with a lack of time and headspace to process and mitigate the impacts. We have to understand that it is the modern workplace, not a lack of resilience, that makes us all so stressed.

Why is stress so prevalent?

Let's remember that 79 per cent of us are disengaged from our jobs. Disengagement has direct consequences for the level of stress we feel, with disengaged employees reporting feelings of stress at a rate up to 83 per cent higher than engaged employees.

Stress and disengagement go hand in hand, with one fuelling the other. Many employees feeling high levels of stress will disengage, partly as a protective mechanism, as the body cannot and does not want to experience ongoing and increasing stress response.

Our stress response is meant to be exactly that. A response. A reaction to a moment in time or a specific situation. Our bodies are used to and can handle this level of stress response, and this isn't harmful to us, as discussed in the previous chapter. However, stress becomes unhelpful when it is chronic and prolonged. Our stress response isn't meant to be continually activated for long periods of time, and when we are experiencing chronic stress, our bodies will disengage or switch off from the situation. This acts as a protective mechanism to try to bring some equilibrium to our minds and bodies.

This is often why chronic stress can lead to depression. We stay stressed and uncomfortable for so long that our bodies and brains disengage and literally depress those mechanisms and so, instead of feeling chronic stress, we feel ... nothing. There is also a social element that links stress and depression. When we are very stressed, we tend to withdraw and isolate as we have no energy left to engage in mood-boosting and rewarding activities. This lack of fun and connection in our lives leads us to experience low mood. What's that saying? All work and no play makes Jack a dull boy? Well, in this case, all stress and no let-up makes Jack a depressed boy. With 80 per cent of workers feeling stress on the job and more than half reporting they need support in better managing stress,[3] the implications for the mental health of all employees are huge.

Making it work

Of course, stress in the workplace is not our only source of stress. Stress is being maintained at a constant low level by the way that we live our lives, as we try to cram more into every minute and try to keep everyone happy, while increasing pressure on ourselves daily. It's a real challenge – one we as a human race are failing to overcome.

Although work may not be the only source of stress, it is often the fall guy, and we channel all of our frustrations around being stressed into work. Work is the part we can put down, especially if we benefit from paid sick leave. If we don't have to lose out financially, then it can be easier to put work down for a short time when we cannot stop other areas of stress in our lives. We cannot stop being a parent, a child or a carer. We cannot stop being responsible, and we can suddenly be side-swiped by physical and mental health issues. In among all of this, work is the bit we can temporarily put down, and so we do.

We probably all know someone who has been signed off work with stress; it may even have been us. There is a supporting pattern within healthcare whereby getting signed off with stress is an easy win for GPs, and no wonder an easy win is needed. In 2018 a report of more than a thousand GPs in the UK found that over 40 per cent of appointments were made by people seeking support for their mental health, with two-thirds of GPs reporting a year-on-year increase. With ten-minute appointments remaining the norm in the UK, despite being acknowledged as too short to be effective,[4] GPs need a quick way to support patients. Although it may not provide a long-term solution, signing someone off with stress certainly deals with the patient sitting in front of them, and many are grateful for the reprieve a break will offer them. This is why, in the UK, stress continues to be one of the main causes of short- and long-term absence in the workplace, with up to 90 per cent of organizations reporting some stress-related absence among their employees.[5]

To recap. Stress is common. It is widely accepted. Work is the part we can put down when everything else becomes too heavy to carry, and we can obtain stress-related sickness absence from work easily (certainly in the UK). Surely, a bit of time off will offer us the solution we seek?

Sadly not.

Time off is not a cure for stress. Although we may benefit from a reprieve, we need to adapt and challenge our current way of being in order to minimize the uncomfortable stress levels we are experiencing. Being continually signed off with stress only reinforces the message that our current role is the problem and that we need a break from it, rather than encouraging us to explore ways to be happy, healthy, safe and engaged in the workplace. We have placed the emphasis onto the role, rather than look at pragmatic solutions. There are so many stressors in the way we live our day-to-day life, all of which can either help or hinder our experience, and impact us at work. One of these stressors may even be in your hand right now.

Not-so-smartphones

We can get a bit jaded about the advice around smartphones and the importance of disconnecting, but there is a reason why these messages are continually repeated. There is no denying that some elements of connectivity are necessary in the modern working world. I personally benefit hugely from having a sat nav in my pocket, given I have no sense of direction.

However, smartphones are ironically named because they are changing how our brains work, and definitely not for the better. This isn't a generic 'phones are good' or 'phones are bad' message. I want you to have the information you need in order to make good decisions. That's it. By understanding exactly why different technologies impact our brains in certain ways, you know what to tweak during tough times. Our stress levels will fluctuate, and how we engage in our technology should change with it to best support our mental health and the underpinnings of health and wellbeing at work.

Brain-blocking

Deep thinking – for example focusing on one topic and absorbing and processing information about one thing at a time – is exercise for our brain. Thinking in this way prevents feelings of overwhelm, as we clear the clutter of our minds and deal with thoughts and problems one at a time.

Social media prevents deep thinking from occurring. Instead, we experience information overload as we repeatedly scroll and absorb too much information for our brains to handle. Imagine the difference between your brain seeing what is in a spotlight (deep thinking) and what is covered in a wide floodlight (information overload). We used to allow our brains to get bored, and it was during this time we would process and absorb information. It was also during this time that we would often be at our most creative, experiencing 'aha' moments while staring out of the window, or doodling in a notepad. These moments are becoming increasingly rare as we occupy this space with scrolling. If you are one of the 77 per cent of employees accessing social media while working,[6] you are robbing yourself of the chance to safely engage in your surroundings and your work.

In 2019 Silicon Valley designer Aza Raskin issued an apology to society in an article in *The Times* newspaper for his role in smartphone addiction. Raskin was the inventor of the 'infinite scroll', whereby we can move through pages and pages of information without needing to click a refresh or next page button. This ability to endlessly scroll has undoubtedly contributed to the three hours per day the average Brit spends scrolling through social media apps on their phone. If you think that's a lot, one in five of us is clocking up more than five hours a day in scrolling time. Don't kid yourself that you are learning and absorbing news when digital amnesia is real, and the technology is designed to distract not enhance your brain function. Aside from the wasted time, though, where's the harm in a bit of scrolling?

All the images we see and information we absorb need to be processed by the brain, regardless of how important or meaningful it is to us. Continually overloading our brain through mindless scrolling impacts the motivational systems in the brain. Information overload will demotivate us and mean we can struggle to get going on even the simplest tasks. We are trapped in a cycle. As our brains struggle and want to feel a sense of achievement and avoid boredom, we reach for our phones. We are trapping ourselves into a system of shorter attention span and minimal motivation. No wonder we are struggling to engage in work when we are carrying our number one distractor in the palms of our hands. We are never far away from it, with 90 per cent of smartphone users keeping their phones within arm's reach 24/7.

HHSE boost: Stop!

Start by stopping. Literally. If you are reaching for your phone, stop yourself and ask what your intention is in that moment. Do you need a distraction? Are you bored? Would something else serve you better in those few moments?

Monitor why and when you are on your phone and try to drop one or two of those habits. If you are stuck in a boring meeting, or are prepping your workstation, then deliberately stay away from your phone and see what your brain does.

I recently worked with a senior executive who told me their screen time was out of control. They believed it was due to email overload and working too hard and so I asked to see their phone. The apps told me a different story. Their social media apps alone were clocking up over three hours per day. They didn't believe me. They said they briefly checked social media while on their phone while doing other tasks, but they had no idea how many minutes were being swallowed up at a time. I said, 'Do you think you're addicted to your phone?' They replied, 'Of course not!' I said, 'Perfect – do you mind if I pop it in my bag for the rest of the session?' They couldn't do it. They lasted 12 minutes out of the hour and were visibly uncomfortable throughout. Even though we were in a coaching session and they weren't going to be on their phone, just being separated from it brought them out in a cold sweat.

These apps know what they are doing. They want your data. That's their sole objective. They're not there to entertain or amuse you. They are there to entice you. I genuinely think in years to come we will look back and wonder why on earth we told some AI system somewhere every little detail about us (for free!), all so that we could have stuff we don't want or need sold back to us. But until then, you need a realistic view of your phone. Everything about it is designed to keep you on it for as long as possible. It's not a weakness to use your phone; you're being trained to do so. Next time you wonder why you never have enough time for you, or you feel overwhelmed or stressed, then know that the device in your hand is deliberately set up to stop you doing anything other than scroll.

Not so rewarding

In theory, we get it. But why is it that phones are so addictive? Surely I can master this … can't I? Human brains are reward-based. If we do something and receive a reward, our brain will want to do that thing again. Social media, smartphone and app usage not only impacts our motivation but also messes with our reward systems.

While apps like Instagram have been shown to boost dopamine, the sheer number of times we use them means we are finding it harder and harder to get a reaction and a subsequent dopamine hit. We previously worried about the impact of social media by focusing on the downsides of comparison and fear of missing out (FOMO), both of which are very valid concerns as they have a significant impact on our mood. But the deeper impacts are happening on a level we cannot see. These apps are literally rewiring our brains to be demotivated and less rewarded. Chamath Palihapitiya, former Vice President of User Growth at Facebook, explains that the short-term, dopamine-driven feedback loops created by social media activate the same neural pathways as cocaine and slot machine addiction.[7] Like all addictions, the higher the usage, the higher the dosage needed to obtain the same hit.

Our constant activation of these neural pathways means we get more dopamine out of social media than many interactions in our real lives. Social media is dampening the joy and reward we would otherwise get out of real-life engagements. If you have been struggling to get motivated or get going on a task that's because, from a brain perspective, the greater and more instant reward will be your phone.

In a world where we are constantly accessing our dopamine and messing with the receptors in our brain, we almost need excessive stress to get anything done. We won't be sparked or motivated by the task in itself; we need our stress response to be triggered just to kick us into action.

This is about as relaxing as it sounds! Constantly needing to be stressed to achieve anything in your life? That's not fun, and there are practical implications. Needing to run out of clothes before you do laundry. Needing to be late before you finally leave the house. Needing an imminent deadline before you get around to that report. It all adds up to a far more stressful lifestyle than it needs to be.

Living in this constant state of stress response leads us to almost become stress seekers. We have numbed our responses to the point where we need those familiar, if uncomfortable, panicky feelings of sympathetic nervous system activation to complete day-to-day tasks. We live our lives with a constant drive for a dopamine boost and a *need* for stress. When it comes to being happy, healthy, safe and engaged, social media has the ability to damage all four underpinnings of good wellbeing.

Using my smartphone for good

We can convince ourselves that our smartphone is our friend. We download mindfulness and calorie-counting apps, maybe even some workplace productivity apps, and convince ourselves that our phones are helpful. They can be. But we have to consider when and why we are using our phones. If we are using our smartphones to stop ourselves feeling an unpleasant emotion such as boredom or frustration or because we are struggling to focus, then this means there is a problem. Especially at work.

Don't kid yourself that your phone is a passive being just waiting to help you out. Many of the apps and interfaces are designed to manipulate us into further use. Instagram's notification algorithms will sometimes withhold 'likes' on your posts, so as to deliver them in larger bursts.[8] This is known as 'variable reward scheduling' and is deliberately designed to manipulate our brain's dopamine reward systems. To be clear, these apps know they are manipulating your brain, and are continually varying the 'reward' you get from them to keep you hooked.

If we had complete control of our social media and phone use, then the impact would be far less damaging, but we don't.

I am not saying you have to disconnect for ever (although, to be honest, if I could do one thing for the good of human mental health, it would be to banish social media), but you do need to wake up to the consequences. That innocent-looking device has a lot more control over you and your brain than you realize, and could be undermining every attempt you make to engage in your role, and indeed in your life.

This device explains the continual and increased stress we are experiencing every day. We need to recognize the hold that our phones and scrolling habits have on us, and then make decisions to regain control, especially in times of stress. When we feel overwhelmed and out of control, reducing our phone use is a simple step we can take to feel better.

HHSE boost: Monitor your smartphone use

Monitor your smartphone use over the next week. Look at where you are spending your time and aim to make a 10–15 per cent reduction the following week. What do you notice? Is it easier than you thought? Harder? Can you reduce further? What can you do in that time instead?

Remember your brain responses work as muscles. They need building up and strengthening. You've been pulled in the direction of distraction for a while now; it's going to take practice and deliberate action to pull in the other and increase your focus and concentration. However, it is worth the effort. Once you get back into deep work, you will notice you feel calmer, more content and happier, as the brain reverts to working as it was designed to. Say goodbye to the excessive stress of modern living and say hello to a happy, healthy, safe and engaged brain.

Stress-feeding behaviours

Reaching for our phones is only one of the ways that we aren't supporting ourselves to manage stress well. Often, being stressed leads to behaviours that may alleviate some stress short term but increase stress overall in the long term.

When stressed, we tend to disengage from helpful behaviours such as going to the gym or eating healthily and instead grab some wine, eat some junk food and stay up late watching films. Your poor brain is all over the place by this point. Your parasympathetic nervous system has been depressed, and you've done nothing to give it a healthy boost. You haven't set your brain up to cope well the next day, and the activities we do try to mitigate stress actually make it worse.

The alcohol we consume depresses our parasympathetic nervous system further, meaning we dampen the part of us that could be making us feel better. (This is also why hangovers are so much worse as we get older. With more attacks on our PNS, it takes longer to achieve an equilibrium and recover.) The junk food we eat causes inflammation, aggravating our stress response and causing digestive discomfort and a disruption of the gut microbiome. A healthy gut microbiome alleviates stress and anxiety, and junk food is not supporting our gut health. Not prioritizing sleep means you aren't getting the rest and recovery that you need, leading to a louder amygdala the next day and therefore making you more likely to feel stressed out.

HHSE boost: Reflection

- What are your unhealthy responses to stress?
- Do you ever rebel against your stress – for example stay up later even though you are tired?
- Is there anything you wish to do but stress stops you doing it?

Once you notice the impact of your stress behaviours, make micro changes to resolve them. Try not to jump in and change everything all at once, as this isn't sustainable change and will feel overwhelming. Instead, try small, daily, incremental changes and work those into your daily routine.

Is stress the bad guy?

Not necessarily. There is such a thing as good and positive stress, known as eustress. Eustress sits at the opposite end of the spectrum to distress.

Eustress is a type of stress that motivates, energizes and drives focus, but differentiates itself from distress as there is no element of threat and fear involved. The same stress response is activated in eustress as in distress, but the feeling of the stress and the resulting emotions are vastly different. Eustress results in feelings of excitement and joy. We can switch out distress for eustress using the mindset shift technique explored in the previous chapter where we reframed our stress response as positive and helpful. This reframing keeps us in the state of excitement and joy, and prevents the negative consequences of distress.

When it comes to work, people often talk about a healthy level of stress, a level that engages and encourages us, motivates us, gives us a little oomph to push through a challenge. Eustress is considered a healthy level of stress or pressure. As the pressure increases and becomes less comfortable, then we can begin to tip into unhelpful stress.

A gentle pressure pushes us to do more than we believe we can, and we feel, perform and experience ourselves at our best when we achieve slightly more than we think we can do. I once heard this described as 4 per cent past your comfort zone – for example taking what you think are your limits and pushing a little way past them. However, 4 per cent does not offer much wriggle room, so we can see how slim the margins are before we tip from healthy pressure into unhelpful stress.

Ideally, you want a level of stress that you can quickly disengage from. It can be hard to go from 100 miles per hour to a dead stop, and we are being wildly unrealistic if we expect our brain to just 'switch off' from very stressful events. Remember your last sorely needed week-long vacation where for the first two to three days you were still thinking about work and feeling a bit tense, before you got into it and relaxed? It's hard to go from feeling negatively stressed to zero – we need time to decompress.

This is why we need to rework our approach to work. We cannot work at full throttle, relying on unhealthy habits to sustain a high-stress approach, and then wonder why we can't relax and switch off. Our brains are designed to cope with typical stress responses, for a way of living that no longer exists. We cannot continue to push our brains to work in unhealthy ways and then blame ourselves for not being 'resilient' enough.

We cannot 'out-resilience' our stress response. We cannot fool our brains that we are relaxed and taking it easy, when we are charging through apace. We have to build practices into our working day that support us to flex and not break when we experience extra stress. Nothing we've discussed in this chapter is permanent, and it's not about never using your phone, drinking alcohol or eating junk food ever again. Rather, it's about recognizing the impact that our everyday life is having on our stress levels. We don't feel the way we do at the moment because of lack of resilience or because we don't cope well. We feel the way we feel because we are set up by our lifestyle to feel this way.

Let's stop beating ourselves up for not coping, and instead focus our energy on working well and flexing with the pressures that life throws at us, knowing when to ease up and when to push forward. When you are stressed, know that it's best to support your body through healthy living and as much digital disconnection as you can manage. Then, as your mood fluctuates, your behaviours can, too. Unless we take back some control, we will burn out, which happens when we don't disconnect from stress overload in time, as we will explore in the next chapter.

Reworking our stressful lives

- If you feel you are not coping, it's not you. The world we live in is designed to activate our stress response and disrupt our natural rhythms of motivation and reward.

- It's not about our resilience to tolerate unending stress, and we shouldn't feel we aren't coping if we get overwhelmed at times.

- We can be stressed in all areas of our lives but are sold time off work as a solution, even though work may not be the problem.

- By better understanding our own reactions to stress, we know what to reign in and what to increase in response to higher stress levels in order to protect our health and happiness in work.

8

Burnout

Meet Simon

I finally won a bid that I had been through a gruelling, year-long pitching process for, only to find that I felt precisely nothing when I got the call telling me I had won. In fact, not only did I feel nothing, but I also then thought, 'I can't be bothered.' I started panicking a little. I'd wanted this contract for a year. Why wasn't I even a little bit relieved or excited? Why hadn't I told my boss yet? Why wasn't I popping champagne? This was a huge win for me, but I couldn't summon up any reaction. I felt nothing ... Actually that's not entirely true. I felt nothing but tired. I kept thinking: 'What's wrong with me?'

No one wants to experience burnout. Indeed, following the global trauma of the COVID-19 pandemic, many of us wanted to embrace a fresh start and begin projects and enjoy travel and all the many other elements of living that we were deprived of during lockdowns and social isolation. However, we were tired. Really tired. More than tired. We were out of oomph.

The most impacted pillar of wellbeing was engagement. So many colleagues would say to me that although they considered themselves to be hard workers, with a strong work ethic, they found that they (whisper it!) just didn't care about anything to do with work. This was extremely triggering for employees who wanted to feel grateful, motivated, happy and engaged in their roles but instead found themselves listlessly looking at their to-do lists and upcoming projects and tasks and just ... didn't care. Almost every individual I spoke to was at a loss. What had happened to them? Why couldn't they get up and get going? Why were they looking at projects so dispassionately? What is wrong with all of us feeling this way?

At the time of writing the phenomenon of 'quiet quitting' is taking the world by storm, but the name is misleading. Quiet quitting is not a form of quitting at all; rather the most commonly agreed definition is 'doing your job'. Nothing more, nothing less. We are not 'skiving', or avoiding our work, we are simply no longer going above and beyond or taking on additional projects. In other words, we are doing exactly the job we are paid for. So where is the controversy? As an ex–NHS worker, I know myself just how many business models rely on people going the extra mile. Companies need people to stretch beyond their role, cover shortfalls and work additional hours when crunch time hits. The norm for many companies is to assume that we will step up to the plate and plug gaps in recruitment, skill, knowledge or resource, and so companies continue to underprovide in these areas. I recently consulted for a company and sat in shocked disbelief as their solution to a need for increased productivity was to tell their employees that they all needed to work an additional eight hours a week. Unpaid. Needless to say, that wasn't the strategy they ended up going with once I stepped in.

Quiet quitting is a sign that we are all out of the goodwill that companies have come to take for granted, and the cracks are beginning to show. No longer are we willing to get in early, stay late and cover extra projects. No, we won't work an additional eight hours which we are not contracted for. We're done. We're tired. We have no 'extra' energy to put into anything, let alone our work. So why is quiet quitting resonating with so many of us? What do all of us from completely different backgrounds, roles, companies and industries have in common? We are burned out.

What is burnout?

A colleague summarized burnout beautifully when she turned to me and said, 'You know the fire in your belly? The thing that sparks joy, sets you alight for your day? Burnout is when that flame inside you has literally burned out. There is no fire, no spark, no joy. Just emptiness. Not even emptiness. Just … nothing. There is nothing there.'

Burnout is more than just a feeling. Although not classified as a medical condition, in 2019 the World Health Organization (WHO) recognized burnout in its eleventh revision of the International Classification of Diseases as an occupational (e.g. work-related) phenomenon. Burnout is defined by the WHO as a syndrome resulting from chronic workplace stress that has not been successfully managed.[1] Before we go any further, let's just pause there and take a moment.

In case you were feeling alone and isolated in your unhappiness at work, or thought that there was something wrong with you for not coping well in your role, use this as proof that this isn't a 'you' issue. There is such a widespread problem within the workplace that the WHO had to include a category solely recognizing work-related stress and resulting burnout.

It's important to recognize that we are not alone and most of us will experience a degree of burnout in our lives. There are good reasons behind those feelings and good solutions to support us. Fully understanding burnout is the best way to protect and heal yourself from it.

Within the WHO classification, there are three key components to burnout:

1 feelings of energy depletion or exhaustion
2 increased mental distance from one's job/feelings of negativism or cynicism related to one's job
3 reduced professional efficacy.

Interestingly, the WHO classification of burnout refers specifically to the occupational context and explicitly states that this classification should not be applied to experiences in other areas of life. However, like everything else, we cannot neatly separate out chunks of our lives and expect them to not touch or cross over.

Although we may all be fed up of thinking about the COVID-19 pandemic and want to put it behind us, we cannot ignore its ongoing impact. COVID-19 changed the face of burnout. Research found that COVID-19 caused a level of burnout typically associated with extensive and chronic unmanaged work-related stress. This means burnout is no longer just a work issue.

We don't need to look too hard to understand why the pandemic may have initiated burnout. More than half of the global workforce worked from home during the pandemic.[2] We were not 'working from home' in the typical sense. We were being forced to stay at home while trying to work.

Those who had to juggle home schooling and work simultaneously faced a, frankly ridiculous, pressure and unrealistic expectation of delivery, with next to no support. If you were going into your workplace every day, you faced additional uncertainty around personal safety and additional complications around childcare as schools and day centres closed. The constant change, the high levels of anxiety, the continual uncertainty meant the challenges were never-ending and, as such, day-to-day life became exhausting.

For many of us, the pandemic changed our roles – whether this was the way we had to work, the way we felt about going to work, the way we were treated at work. Even if, fundamentally, nothing changed within their roles, everything around them changed. On paper, it may have looked the same, but to experience it was very different.

Am I burned out?

Being able to recognize burnout is key to building and maintaining our HHSE status. Although it can feel scary to admit to burnout, actually doing so offers a form of release and freedom. Instead of beating ourselves up for not achieving, striving or planning with boundless energy, we can recognize where we need to put our energy. We can spot what is burning us out and, excitingly, we can reconnect with what sparks us, setting us alight with energy and enthusiasm. Spotting burnout in its various forms allows us to manage and recover from it and boost our HHSE scores. For many, admitting to burnout feels like defeat, but in fact it is a necessary reset to get us back on the right path to workplace wellbeing.

The three core elements of burnout, as defined by the WHO, have many identifiable symptoms underneath them – for example, energy depletion or exhaustion which could be emotional, physical or both. Exhaustion can be responsible for other symptoms such as forgetfulness or impaired concentration. Ironically, burnout can lead to insomnia, meaning when we feel most exhausted, we struggle to get restful and restorative sleep, which impacts our mood and makes us irritable.

As we know from our stress response, we may notice changes in appetite during burnout and a reliance on stimulants such as caffeine, alcohol and drugs. Due to exhaustion, we may change our diet to meet convenience rather than health needs, turning to short-term reward foods with high sugar, fat and salt.

The increased mental distance from one's job, or feelings of negativity or cynicism towards one's role, is also a symptom of burnout and it explains the feeling of simply not caring. It's not that we are bad employees who don't care about our work; it's that we are too burned out to connect to our role.

When we do work, we feel less effective in our roles. This can be perceived or actual ineffectiveness, but either way it is unpleasant to feel as though we are trying but not getting anywhere. This feeling leads to pessimism about what we can achieve and we lose confidence and begin to doubt our abilities. It is also common to experience anxiety before starting work, as we feel less capable and less sure that we can complete what we need to do. This loss of confidence leads us to procrastinate more. We'll look at procrastination and the role it plays in preventing HHSE behaviours later, but we rarely procrastinate out of laziness, yet often berate ourselves for exactly that.

HHSE boost: How do you feel?

Take a moment to consider how you have been feeling lately. Have you been experiencing any of those three areas of burnout? Are you exhausted? Disengaged? Have you been feeling less productive and effective than usual? Is it possible that you have been feeling some degree of burnout?

Think about that fire in your belly. Is it roaring? Glowing? Sparking? Or has it been snuffed out? Start by stopping and consider what is going on for you right now.

How would you finish this sentence: 'Out of ten my current level of burnout is …'?

I can't tell if I am tired, stressed or burned out

Tiredness, stress and burnout can look very similar. If you receive an email or get given a task and you suddenly feel overwhelmed and tearful, then any one of these states could be the cause.

Think of a spectrum which starts with tired, moves through stress and ends in burnout. It doesn't follow that tiredness will automatically lead to stress, or that stress will automatically lead to burnout. But, if left unmanaged, then our experiences will move along the spectrum, and if we leave tiredness and stress completely unmanaged, then the result will be burnout.

I'm tired. You're tired. We're all tired

It's easy to dismiss tiredness. After all, aren't we all a bit tired now and then? Tiredness typically will have an explanation. It could be a poor night's sleep or a physically exhausting day that leads you to feel tired. Typically, tiredness can be resolved with rest. An early night, a nap, a quieter and more restful day or two and you're back to feeling more you.

Fatigue sits at the more extreme end of tiredness. Fatigue can result from a variety of different health conditions, or from pushing through tiredness without mitigating the impact. Often, our bodies experience fatigue as a little warning sign. Say you were on a long walk, there would be points where you'd feel tired and need to stop, maybe have a drink and a snack, and then you could progress. Fatigue would be when you were very low on energy, able but struggling to continue, and all enjoyment had stopped. Our emotional response is a critical differentiator between the two. Typically, when tired, we are still able to enjoy ourselves. We often find a reserve of energy from somewhere, be that a second wind, or a fourth coffee, and we can push through and still fully engage in the activity or task at hand. Fatigue is different. When fatigued we are really just gritting our teeth and pushing through, not taking much enjoyment out of a situation and hoping it ends soon. Once finished, we often need a deeper and longer period of rest before we fully recover.

So, tired means a temporary dip in energy, which doesn't have too strong an emotional impact and is easily recoverable, usually through sleep and rest. Fatigue is a larger drain on our energy and we need a more intensive period of recovery in order to feel fully revived. From a work perspective, you can still work when tired and fatigued, although the more tired we become, the more impact we will see on energy, motivation and productivity.

Stress is different again. As we know from our understanding of the stress response, stress has many impacts, both physically and psychologically, and tiredness and fatigue can be symptoms of stress, but can also be the cause. Continual tiredness and fatigue can make life more challenging and harder to deal with, and we can be more irritable and struggle to concentrate, making us feel more stressed.

Stress tends to be situational specific. A particular situation will be stressing us out. It could be a project or deadline at work; it could be a relationship issue; it could be being stuck in traffic when on our way to an important appointment. When the stressor is resolved then our stress levels decrease.

Burnout is very different from feeling tired, stressed or fatigued. Burnout means having nothing left in the tank. You have no reserve, no second wind, and it doesn't go away once a situation improves.

Habituating to burnout

We think we'd see something as dramatic as burnout on the horizon, but it's not always easy to identify. Because stress is the underlying cause of burnout, we often habituate to our stress response, and the slow creep to burnout can be insidious. We won't have a single event and immediately feel overwhelmed and burned out, and this can make burnout harder to spot and mitigate. The more we habituate to feeling stressed, the higher our threshold for continuing stress, and the harder it is to focus and pinpoint what is causing us issues and where we need to put some of our remaining energy into recovery, before it's all burned out.

Our bodies are very clever, and as we approach burnout, we will be given lots of cues. Have you ever been really busy and then developed a headache or a head cold, or made lots of weekend plans only to end up having a weekend not doing much other than staying in bed? Rather than thank our bodies for these helpful cues pointing to a little overwhelm, stress and need for rest along the route to potential burnout, we take painkillers, resent the 'wasted' weekend, and crack on.

We need to tune into the cues and get to know our baseline energy levels so that we can monitor changes and understand what we need to put in place. Your body will move you from tiredness, through fatigue and all the way through a prolonged stress response before you reach burnout. That's a lot of opportunities to catch and mitigate burnout.

HHSE boost: Start monitoring your energy spend

Imagine your energy is money. Let's say you get £10 for your whole day. You cannot borrow from yesterday or tomorrow and you cannot go overdrawn. You wake up in the morning with £10. How quickly do you get through your money? What activity costs you the most money? On a good day, your daily activities such as showering and brushing your teeth shouldn't cost you more than a few pence, but on a tough day, these activities alone may blow half your budget. For the next week or so, monitor your 'spend'. If you find that by 11 a.m. every day you are through your money, then this is telling you something about your level of burnout.

Also make note of what gives you extra money. Some activities will refresh and replenish your energy, giving you a little top-up. What activities are giving you a little extra? Remember to monitor every activity, no matter how mindless or 'cheap' it seems. Everything we do costs us energy, and even the little spends add up.

I made big changes … but I'm still tired

The so-called Great Resignation where people left their jobs in droves was driven by many different factors, and we cannot dismiss collective burnout as one of the factors that led a record 4.53 million Americans to quit their jobs in November 2021[3], with a further 20 million quitting in the first half of 2022.[4]

As we know though from the basic principles of this book, reactive quitting doesn't solve existing problems. Unless you do the work and understand exactly what you are looking for, then quitting will not address the issues. Seventy-two per cent of workers regret the decision to leave their old job as the new role did not match expectations or hopes, and nearly half of those who quit said they wished they could have their old job back. As predicted, the Great Resignation did not resolve the issues we face, or make us happier, healthier, safer or more engaged.

The collective burnout we feel following the pandemic is understandable, and it explains why we have been feeling exhausted. Some situational elements may have improved as we, hopefully, continue to put the pandemic behind us, but there is still more work to do.

Of course, the path to burnout existed before the pandemic. In the 1970s the term *karoshi* – which translates as 'death from overwork' – was coined in Japan. This country is often used to illustrate an extreme work culture, but the reality is that we now see the unrealistic and unsustainable demands placed on workforces across the globe. The Organisation for Economic Co-operation and Development (OECD) stated that, globally, 10 per cent of employees work 50 hours or more per week,[5] in a report published alongside the WHO warning us that working over 55 hours per week poses a serious health hazard.[6] The idea of hard work being honourable and deserving of high praise has swept over us like a giant wave and we feel a clash of values as we want to work hard and be seen as a valuable employee, but also recognize the damage of overwork and increased risk of burnout.

It can be hard to change a culture cemented by multiple generations, and we need to be mindful that the pressure to work we feel is not just ours but the inherited pressure of thousands of employees before us. We are not just experiencing one individual company's culture but the deeply cemented culture of an entire country. Japan has the lowest use of annual leave in the world, with many employees citing peer pressure and not wanting to be viewed badly as reasons for not taking their paid leave. Times are changing, however. In 2018 the Japanese government passed its 'Work Style Reform Legislation', which includes enforcing paid leave, and today we see Japan's younger generations taking more of their annual leave or paid time off to travel and explore. A particularly poignant Buddhist ceremony known as Yukyu Joka ('paid holiday purification') was held in Tokyo to mourn the unused vacation days of Japan's employees, and to encourage everyone to foster a positive attitude towards using their paid time off. Actions like these will persist in influencing and changing work culture around us, but we need to recognize this is a slow-turning wheel, and we cannot wait for external forces to give us permission to make changes. We need to take control and prioritize our health and happiness because the world around us doesn't.

The WHO definition of burnout provides a good insight into the phenomenon and helps us recognize it, but there is another very important element of burnout that is commonly felt but rarely discussed. It can be a complete blocker to increasing HHSE at work, yet it won't be covered in your performance reviews. What is this secret side of burnout? Anger.

The raging truth about burnout

We may think anger has no place in burnout. After all, we have a familiar image of someone who is burned out. Someone sat with their head in their hands, or lying in bed, eyes open but unable to get up and get going. All of the images we carry of burnout suggest exhaustion, and anger, being a high-energy emotion, can feel out of place. However, anger has a fundamental impact on us.

Part of the reason why burnout is so damaging, so noxious, so much to cope with, is because most people truly care about their work. If we didn't, it wouldn't affect us so much. We want to do a good job, and we want to work hard. But we are thwarted. Hindered. Held back. We burn out because we have so much to offer a company and no channel to put it through. We burn out because we are utterly fed up. In fact, we are raging.

Meet Claire

When I first joined the company, I was so excited about my role. I was told in interview that I would be given a blank slate, and I was literally fizzing with ideas. I was impatient to start, and I told my partner that, even if I didn't get the job, I was going to write a strategic paper and send it to them because I was so enthused by the role! Fast-forward three years and I am broken. It's been three years of being told 'no'. It's been three years of the company citing budget constraints and an inability to procure more headcount and endless other reasons why I cannot do the job I was hired to do.

I love innovative solutions, and they don't need to be expensive. Part of the fun is the creativity challenge of a limited budget … but I do need *some* resource! Over the last few months, I have become increasingly exhausted, but also really angry. The expectations of the company don't change, and employees look to me to solve problems and I can't. I feel utterly powerless, and I disappoint someone every day, through no fault of my own. I feel as though I am constantly moaning or being negative, but I honestly cannot progress in my role. I have no other job to go to and no energy to job hunt, but I am at the point where I am going to leave because I feel suffocated. I feel as though I was told I had the freedom to fly to the moon in the interview, but then from day one someone clipped my wings.

I am a really positive person, and yet this job has made me feel burned out and depleted in every way, but more than that, I am SO angry! I feel wound up all the time and can't relax. It's so weird because I am constantly tired but also really wired. I am so fed up that I will be financially vulnerable when all I want to do is the job I was hired for! I feel my sparkle dull a little more each day. I am so frustrated I don't know whether to laugh or cry or shout or scream or punch something. I am thwarted at every turn and cannot succeed where I am.

What struck me when talking to Claire was the split of emotion. On the one hand, she was broken. Utterly depleted. Spent. Yet on the other she had a lot of energy which was expended on anger. Claire felt she needed to leave because she was struggling so much yet she bitterly resented the situation. All Claire wanted was to work hard.

Working with individuals like Claire, I have noticed patterns. Many employees felt thwarted and even reported feeling they'd taken a step back and were doing work they had previously done at least five-ten years ago in their careers. Thwarted employees feel increasingly deskilled and have no opportunity for development or growth. Both company and individual expectations of roles remain high, meaning employees have daily reminders of what they want, but are unable, to do. It isn't intentional thwarting, often lack of resource is cited as the main issue, but the outcome is the same.

A survey of seven thousand office workers from ten European countries found that 89 per cent sought fulfilment as a top priority in their roles and also found that 97 per cent of workers were feeling frustrated.[7] What odds does that hold for disengagement and burnout, when nearly every office worker is experiencing a degree of frustration?

Employees like Claire are wasted if not given the opportunity to shine. These employees want to contribute and make a real difference. When there is a disconnect between the work we want to do and know is needed, and that which we are being asked to do, we become disengaged and angry. This is an increasingly common situation in companies that are not supporting the growth and development of employees. As we saw in the previous chapter, the importance of growth and a healthy pressure supports us to build confidence. Being thwarted in this way will leave us angry and negatively impact our HHSE score.

There is a plus side to this anger, though. As mentioned, anger is an energetic emotion. When we feel burned out, we feel utterly depleted, as though we cannot move forward because we have no energy. But it takes a lot of energy to feel angry.

If you are currently feeling angry and fed up with your situation, take heart because that means you have some energy at your disposal. You can recover from burnout, and it doesn't need to be high energy or dramatic. You can put the energy you have into your recovery and take your first steps out of burnout.

Can't I just ignore it?

I'm afraid not. Burnout won't just disappear on its own.

Sometimes we feel ourselves burning out and we put off facing it thinking, 'I'll deal with that this weekend' or 'When the holidays come, then I'll really take time off to relax.' Burnout is not something that you can push against or ignore and hope that it will go away. Nor will it run to your schedule, fitting in when most convenient to you. Although self-care activities are a fantastic way to take care of our wellbeing, we also cannot fix chronic and prolonged stress in one weekend, no matter how many candles we light and Epsom salt baths we run.

The fact that there is no quick fix should not be misinterpreted as there being no fix at all. Completely recovering from burnout is relatively straightforward, but we need a plan.

Plans, tools and strategies

The key to managing burnout is exactly that. *Managing* it. You need a plan. Again, this is quite a big ask when you are feeling burned out and are not actually sure you can get out of bed or are filled with an impotent rage. However, this plan is different. This isn't about creating a harsh and aggressive to-do list. The planning involved in burnout recovery is gentle, and the execution of those plans is even gentler. This is a cosy, restorative and gentle hug at a time when you need it most.

All the information and techniques outlined throughout this book are designed to get and keep you happy, healthy, safe and engaged, which is the antithesis of burnout. Everything you learn and put into practice will act as a buffer against stress and burnout, and support you to have your best day at work.

If you are feeling burned out right now, then there are some immediate actions you can put into practice, and I really recommend taking a few minutes every day to do so wherever you can. You will start to feel more energized and more 'you' straight away.

Five top tips for burnout recovery

1 **Put boundaries in place.** If someone collapses in a crowd, what's the first thing you do? You step in front of them, face the crowd, spread your arms out so no one can pass and say, 'Move back, give them space.' In other words, you put a boundary in place between the individual and the people around them, and give yourself space to support the person that needs it. Boundaries are our superpower when it comes to burnout, and you need to give yourself

plenty of space in order to work out what is happening and what you need. We'll be exploring effective boundaries in more detail later on in this book, but your immediate steps need to be to put some boundaries in place to protect you while you work out what you need.

2 **Delete what you can.** Go through your diary and delete, move, postpone or cancel whatever you can to give yourself breathing space. We can struggle to do this as we feel guilty, but don't. If you are burned out, then people aren't getting the best of you anyway, so push back and reschedule whatever you can to give yourself a clear calendar. Imagine you have flu. You wouldn't think, 'Oh, I'd better turn up to that meeting anyway,' if you were vomiting and contagious, so use the same principle here. If you are burned out then your health is impacted and you need rest. Clear everything you can for the foreseeable future.

3 **Write a future-focused list.** This list will consist of all the things you will do when you are not burned out. Staying future focused and remembering that burnout is temporary is really important, and writing a list of things you will do when you are energized and feeling well again puts you in the right frame of mind. This definitely isn't a work to-do list so don't add projects and chores; instead, think of things you will do for you when you have a bit more energy. It could be cooking your favourite meal. Watching your favourite film. Going back to that spin class that you love. Visiting a favourite childhood spot. Whatever it is, start making a list of enjoyable activities that are meaningful to you and that appeal for when you have more energy.

4 **Clear the clutter.** I don't mean physical, but mental. Leave your phone alone. Don't go on social media, avoid the news, don't take on board any more information than

you absolutely have to. This can also mean cancelling social plans while you catch your breath. Remember, this isn't a long-term approach, this is a crisis response, so let go of guilt and pressure. You will socialize and reconnect with the world again, but in this moment, you need to relax and clear your mind; giving yourself more to process will not support you.

5 **Be honest wherever you can.** Some people in your life will not be useful to you at this moment. These are the people who, if you tell them you are burned out, will say, 'Oh, tell me about it!' and spend the next 40 minutes talking about how tired they are and dumping their problems on you. Also, if you have people in your life who aren't up for a chat about mental states and dismissively tell you to 'cheer up' or 'practise gratitude', although well meaning, they are not the ones you need right now. But there will be some people who will be useful, and you need to be honest and tell them how you are feeling – your partner, your manager, your colleagues, your friends. People who will understand and support you and will help you to recover. When we tell people, it prevents them unwittingly piling on pressures or suggesting activities when you just feel wiped. Also, if your children are old enough, then don't be afraid to tell them that you are a little low on energy. We worry about protecting our kids, but it's never too early to start a conversation about being HHSE and role-modelling great practices. Perhaps you can all have a duvet day together, watching films and eating yummy food. Whoever needs to know in your life, take a deep breath and tell them.

Where next?

That last one around being honest can feel a big ask. Opening up and being vulnerable can be scary, and being authentic about our situation can feel unnatural. We may be particularly unsure how to do this at work.

Being authentically you in the workplace is the most important action to achieve true HHSE status. We cannot be truly happy, healthy, safe or engaged if we are pretending to be someone else. In truth, stress, burnout and a lack of safety can all be mitigated through being authentic but we can feel stumped. How am I authentic? Where do I start? How much is too much 'me' to share?

The next chapter is going to explore how you can use authenticity as the supercharged power to boost your HHSE score and experience true wellbeing in any role.

Reworking burnout

- Burnout is an authentic and recognized condition which follows prolonged and unmanaged workplace stress.
- We are all more vulnerable to burnout, even if our role hasn't significantly changed, as the pandemic has caused burnout levels previously only associated with the workplace.
- Being thwarted in work can lead to burnout and feelings of rage, which is a source of energy that can be harnessed to support us to feel better.
- Boundaries are a safety net to protect us from further burnout.
- We cannot fix burnout with short-term solutions such as a bath or a long weekend, but burnout is fixable nonetheless.

9

Being Your Authentic Self at Work

A job interview can feel like an audition. You go in front of the director and talk about previous parts you've played. You usually need some pretty good reviews, and it helps if you've played on some of the major stages. Once you get the job, then off you go. Perform. Dazzle! Your critic ratings will be in at the end of the year.

If we don't feel our authentic selves at work, then we are playing a part. We're under the spotlight, trying to learn the lines, characteristics and mannerisms that we believe our character should have. Sometimes it can be quite fun to act a part at work, but after a while it can become problematic.

Actors become exhausted acting the same part night after night. It doesn't matter how much they love their role – eventually they become fatigued trying to access the same motivation and energy to put into their performance on a daily basis. Also, many actors report a disconnect and sense of isolation that happens when the character they are playing is very different from them and their personality. No one ever gets to know the real person behind the façade of the role.

Do you ever feel as though you're acting a part at work? As though you auditioned for your role and now you have to perform on a stage with an audience? Do you feel like *you* when you are working?

Being authentic at work is fundamental to being happy, healthy, safe and engaged, yet it is challenging. Being authentic makes us feel exposed and vulnerable. After all, if we play a part and someone doesn't like us, or thinks we aren't doing a good job, then we can think, 'Oh well, that's not really me,' and so our faking it can protect us. However, it can also diminish us. Unless we are authentic at work, we cannot build confidence, engage in our role, build psychological safety and ultimately be happy in our workplace.

How authentic are we at work?

A UK-based survey revealed that more than one in five (22 per cent) of us feels we can't be our true selves in our current job or career.[1] That figure rose to 30 per cent of Gen Z adults (those aged between 18 and 25 years). However, it isn't that these individuals lack the ability to be authentic, as 85 per cent revealed that they felt more at ease expressing themselves outside work. More than two-thirds of working adults feel that being authentic in the workplace would lead to greater job satisfaction, while an overwhelming 90 per cent feel expressing individuality in working life is important.

So, we recognize the importance of being authentic but we aren't following through with action. Why not?

Being authentically ourselves in work is a direct challenge and contradiction to the many generations before us who believed that we should separate out our work self and our home self. People talked about adopting a professional persona and trying not to stand out too much. There was a belief that to progress in the workplace you should try to blend in as much as possible and act as your 'professional self' at all times, never letting the façade slip.

Meet Melissa

I'm the managing director of a major supermarket chain, but I started on the checkouts. I remember my very first day on the job we had an induction with our manager who said, 'No one cares what sort of day you are having or what is going on for you. You need to smile, be polite and do your job. That's it.' I was 15 years old at the time, and I carried that throughout my career for decades. I was too young to realize that what they meant was they didn't want you taking your bad day out on customers. I didn't realize it was OK to be myself with colleagues. I never asked questions or told anyone if I was struggling or didn't understand something. No matter what was going on in my personal life, for years I put a smile on my face and did my job. I'd see other colleagues chat with each other about their personal lives and I would think, 'How unprofessional.' I didn't make friends at work. I didn't know how to connect with anyone. This wasn't a huge problem until I was promoted to manager and I had no idea how to lead my team. I didn't know any of them, and they knew nothing about me. When people don't know you, they fill in the gaps about you, and they're rarely accurate or flattering! I had to learn how to be my authentic self, not the two-dimensional version I'd always shown at work. Nowadays I am 100 per cent me at work, and the connections and friendships I have are really important to me. I wish I could go back to 15-year-old me and tell her how important it is to be yourself, to ask questions, to tell people if you need a little extra help. I think I still carry a bit of that early experience with me and have to push myself to be authentic, but it's so worth it.

Melissa's early experiences are indicative of the workplace many of us grew up with, and remain embedded in the culture of the companies we work for. This adds to the challenge of being authentic at work. People around us will have different experiences and expectations, and will have worked in different company cultures, all of which will contribute to how comfortable they feel, and how comfortable they make you feel, with being authentic.

Sometimes we don't have a choice about how others see us at work. People can make huge assumptions about our roles and therefore the type of person who is in them. I can't tell you the number of times I have heard people talk about a certain type of role and followed it up with 'But actually they're a really lovely person,' as though they are surprised that someone could be in that role but also have a great personality.

These assumptions mean we quickly get pushed into a role or a part that we feel we have to play and once these parts are established, we can feel very stuck and unsure how to get out of them.

Meet Argyll

My boss had this weird perception of me from the word go. She introduced me to people in ways that I didn't recognize. I felt uncomfortable but also as though there was no good way to correct her as often these introductions were to her peers or the rest of the team. I felt a bit panicky. I think she was trying to be nice and encouraging but she would go up to the team and say things like 'This is Argyll, he's one serious high-flyer' or 'Everyone be nice to Argyll because one day he'll be your boss!' She sort of made me out to be this ambitious, ruthless leader, and I felt I had to act that way, when in reality I have no leadership ambition at all. I'm a naturally inquisitive person, but felt I couldn't ask questions or I'd look incompetent and it would go against this version of me that my boss had introduced to the company. I'd often nod along in conversations as though I understood and then spend hours googling acronyms because I hadn't asked what they meant. I also felt I couldn't engage in any work with the team because my boss had made me sound like I'd step on them just to climb higher, which again is completely against my character and my values. I just didn't feel like me at all.

Argyll's boss was probably trying to give him a confidence boost and set a positive and motivational tone in introducing him to the team. But Argyll also felt he was being used for a different agenda. He felt his introduction posed a 'we're bringing in new blood to shake things up' threat, which made his first encounter with his team challenging, hostile and, most notably, inauthentic.

The power of our work identity

We can get so caught up in how we present ourselves at work that we lose sight of who we really are. Spending so much time in an inauthentic place means we become used to working in that way and we continually disengage, not just from the work, but from ourselves. We lose sight of the person we are and can struggle to cope with changes in that identity, especially if we are put in a role where we can no longer pretend.

Following the birth of her first child, Sophia experienced low mood and was monitored for postnatal depression

(PND). The hope was that it was natural 'baby blues' and that things would settle for Sophia as her baby grew older, but instead things grew steadily worse. Her partner reported that Sophia was completely different from the person he had known before their baby arrived. Sophia was very relaxed and comfortable around the baby, if a little tired at times, and didn't seem to portray the 'typical' PND symptoms.

Before having children, Sophia described herself as having a very 'type A' personality. Sophia strongly associated her self-worth with achievement, was fiercely competitive and liked to move through the world at a whirlwind pace. Sophia's problem was not that she had PND, but the fact that babies move at their own pace and Sophia couldn't rush or control this. Sophia had only two weeks' paid maternity leave at work and took an additional 12 weeks' unpaid leave, but didn't feel ready to return to work when the time came.

When she did return, Sophia no longer had the energy or time to work how she used to and her mental health deteriorated. Before her maternity leave, Sophia was often praised for her presentations, and they would be showcased at very senior meetings. However, her colleagues didn't know that Sophia would stay up until gone 11 p.m. tweaking and perfecting those presentations. They also didn't know that she would regularly skip lunch breaks in order to take on extra work and duties and declined many potentially enjoyable social engagements to dedicate time to her work. Sophia created a superhero identity for herself at work, thriving on the praise and reward of others. Sophia became depressed after having her child because she linked her self-worth with productivity, achievement and admiration from others, and this was taken away from her once she stopped work.

Meet Sophia

I just became a mum. I thought 'anyone can be a mum' whereas my previous role was really only mine. The whole point for me was that at work no one knew how long it took me to do something; they just thought I was really good at my job. I loved that. I loved that people felt I had that ability, as though it was effortless for me. I took on projects that were far above my paygrade because I was trusted to do them. Anyone can be a competitive mum, but you can't pretend you just did all that easily. Like, if I make all my own organic extra-amazing baby food, no one is going to think I just did that effortlessly. I don't want people to know how hard I have to work; I loved it when they thought I was just brilliant. Now I don't have that. I know it's nonsense and ego and what have you, but it's who I am. Now I'm back at work, I feel really uncertain how to act. I don't have the energy to keep up the same standards, but I feel as though they'll all know I was faking before. Losing 'work me' really hurt, and I feel a bit lost without her.

Sophia's experience shows us that the 'work us' is very real and shouldn't be ignored or underestimated. It's a huge part of who we are on a daily basis, and when this is misrepresented, it is hugely challenging to our sense of self and our beliefs about others and the world around us. Sophia had no confidence that she would be accepted as she actually is, having never shown that side of herself before. By going to ridiculous lengths to get more and more work done, Sophia had painted herself into a corner, and was unsure how to act once she returned to work.

Maintaining a false representation of ourselves at work is not sustainable. It is effortful and exhausting and ultimately disengaging as you cannot emotionally connect with success that doesn't feel as though it belongs to you, but rather belongs to a role that you play. A good working relationship requires truth, respect and mutual trust, all of which are essential for effective teamwork and safe, healthy workplace practices.[2]

Gaining confidence through authenticity

During a 2019 book launch event for her *Work Like a Woman* book, British entrepreneur and TV and radio presenter Mary Portas was posed a question about imposter syndrome.

Imposter syndrome, as defined by psychologists Suzanne Imes and Pauline Rose Clance in the 1970s, is the name given to the feeling that we shouldn't be in our role or position at work. It is characterized by a fear of being 'found out' or discovered to be fraudulent in some way. Those struggling with imposter syndrome are often high achievers who are unable to internalize or accept their successes, instead attributing these to luck rather than ability.

Portas replied by saying, 'I don't like the term "imposter syndrome", because isn't that just the typical way we all feel at work? Don't we all have days and weeks where we don't feel good enough or judge ourselves too harshly? I don't think that's "imposter syndrome", I think it's just being at work.'[3]

Her response normalized the way so many of us feel at work, and we can see how a lack of authenticity contributes to feeling this way. Work acts as a magnifying glass for those flaws that we perceive in ourselves and desperately try to hide from the rest of the world. If we try to be the perfect employee all the time, then we will constantly worry about being 'found out' and discovered for being less than perfect.

Being perfect lowers your confidence

The problem with aiming for perfect is that perfection doesn't really exist. There is no such thing as a perfect employee. We are aiming at goalposts that will constantly shift and alter depending on who you ask and under what circumstances. We are making it impossible to win.

We really prize perfectionism in the workplace. It's the sort of attribute that people faux-modestly confess in job interviews when asked about weaknesses. 'Well, I am a bit of a perfectionist,' they say with a pretend eye roll or self-deprecating laugh. If we set ourselves up for 'perfect', then we will always fall short, not because of anything we are doing wrong but because perfect as a measurement doesn't exist. Take parenting. If you ask 100 people what makes the perfect parent, there may be some similarities, but there will be many more differences. Everyone will have their own idea of what perfect means to them. Therefore, if we are trying to prove ourselves as the perfect employee, we cannot ever succeed. Even if we work out what is perfect for our boss, it may not be perfect for the team, the company or for ourselves.

More than being impossible to achieve, perfect blocks authenticity, breeds imposter syndrome and prevents us from ever developing confidence in work.

If ever you've gone to buy a slice of cake from a coffee shop, you'll have noticed that they always present the perfect-looking slice. It's the slice with the most icing and the prettiest topping; it's the most delicious and tempting slice of cake they can present. They obviously do this for a reason – they want you to buy the cake. What they don't do is show you the other side, the burned, messy, crumbly bits of the cake. They don't present you with the slice that someone accidentally dropped. They are selling you the perfect slice of cake, and we buy it.

We are all cakes. As cakes, we all present our best slices to the world, particularly at work. But we need to remember that we are not *slices*. For true confidence, we want those around us to accept the *whole* cake.

The longer we present only the slice, the more compelled we feel to hide the rest of us, and the more we lose confidence. Unless we are authentic at work, we will feel constantly rejected. Our experiences, values, skills and innovations are baked into the whole cake, not just one slice. Without the whole cake we become a one-dimensional shadow of who we actually are. If people only ever show appreciation for the slice, then we will lose confidence in the rest of our cake. Only when we reveal the whole cake are we being authentically us. We learn that people are interested in more than just the slice as they get to know and accept all of us, and this is where we gain true confidence. Remember Melissa? Presenting the slice led to isolation and loneliness, and she couldn't connect with her team. Only by bringing her whole self to work did she develop the connections and confidence needed to lead her team. Being authentic made her an infinitely better employee than the perfect 'slice' she was pretending to be.

Confidence at work comes through the acceptance of the cake, and the more authentic we can be, the more fulfilled we become.

Remember our HHSE score questions? Being authentic means looking forward to going to work, rather than dreading being found out. Being authentic means feeling you can be at your best and that you feel safe and respected. It means you are emotionally connected to your job. Authenticity really is your HHSE superpower. To misquote Marie Antoinette, 'Let them see the cake!'

An authentic feeling

Being your authentic self is not as straightforward as simply saying 'I'll be myself'. We need to reconnect with our values.

Other people's opinions and the experiences we go through may mean that we lose sight of our true values. We can lose track of who we really are, particularly in the workplace. Sometimes our first indicator that something is wrong can be a feeling. Much like Argyll's experience: he knew something was wrong because he felt uncomfortable. It may not be obvious: on paper everything looks fine but the lived experience feels different. Our values are the anchor that brings us back to our authenticity and allow us to reconnect with our whole self at work.

Argyll and I worked together to reconnect him to his values. Argyll considered what being authentic looked like for him and found it was curiosity. Because of others' perception of him, he felt unable to ask questions, which was limiting what he was able to learn. He wasn't feeling stretched or developed, which was really important to him. Argyll challenged himself to ask each of his colleagues at least one question per day, and to answer any questions posed to him with authenticity.

Argyll went into work the next day and his colleague was quietly working on a process. Argyll approached and said, 'Can I ask you about what you are doing?' His colleague looked at him suspiciously and said, 'Why?' Argyll answered honestly: 'I love learning and I haven't had the opportunity to ask many questions since I started. I would really love to understand more about the business and how these processes work.' Argyll's colleague remained a little off-hand, but as he and Argyll began to discuss the process, they both got really enthusiastic about it and Argyll was able to ask many more questions about how this linked to other areas in the business, and he felt his brain click into gear.

Meet Argyll

I felt a new man! I suddenly felt like the real me had walked into the workplace and I was able to ask questions and have conversations with colleagues and make sense of things. I felt so much more 'me' than sitting alone in the office trying to piece it all together, using Google and guesswork. The more I asked, the more people knew I was genuinely interested in their work and I started to feel accepted. I also got a lot more confident asking questions and offering some solutions. I could really see where I could add value and how I linked in with others and their work. Being more me was a game changer.

This is the power of authenticity in action. It connects you to the work you love. By bringing more of himself into work, Argyll was able to engage in the work meaningfully, and he created a sense of psychological safety where he could ask questions and truly connect with his colleagues. Argyll felt happier, healthier, safer and more engaged in his work. This all came through authenticity.

HHSE boost: Reflection

- What can you share with others at work to bring more of your authentic self to the workplace?
- What is one small step, question or action that you could bring into work tomorrow that would feel authentic?
- What difference would being authentic make to how HHSE you feel at work tomorrow?

Working inauthentically is like wearing an uncomfortable sweater every day. It doesn't fit, it doesn't suit you, you don't like the material, and it's unlike anything else you have in your wardrobe. Sometimes we make our own ill-fitting sweater by presenting only a slice, or portraying an image of how we'd like to be seen which we then struggle to maintain. Being authentic means being more comfortable, showing people your true style, and connecting with others who share that with you.

It is so important to be our authentic selves at work, and it is our values that will connect us to our truest selves and what makes us happiest. But what if you've lost sight of your values, or have never really felt you've brought them into the workplace? Where do you start?

Finding your values

Broaden your mindset beyond work and start with what you absolutely and fundamentally know about yourself. For example, let's say you are a passionate believer in equality. What is it about equality that you feel so fired up about? Maybe you feel people should be treated fairly and equally; you feel everyone has a story to share and should be given equal opportunity to be listened to. Maybe you love hearing others' stories, and this satisfies a deeper need within you for community and connection.

In this example, fairness, storytelling and connection are emerging as three core values. Once we identify our values, we can begin seeking opportunities to bring those into our own work. We can do this regardless of the role we are in. Our values form who we are and how we behave, and staying rooted in our values prevents us being forced into play acting an inauthentic role at work. Living our values is the pathway to being happy, healthy, safe and engaged.

HHSE boost: What are your core values?

- What do you feel most strongly about?
- How has this changed over the years, if it has?
- Are you holding other people's values that don't suit you and that you want to let go of?
- Where do you see your values showing up in your everyday work life?
- Where would you like to see them showing up?
- Where do you see clashes between work and your values?
- Have your roles changed along with your values?
- Are you stuck in a past version of you, your roles or your values? What would you like to shift to reconnect your work and your values?

Recognizing your values is the type of work you need to do *before* you quit. Unless you are connected to your values, and understand what really makes your heart sing, you can stumble your way through many different career options and never feel truly satisfied.

I have worked with many individuals who have always held a perception of who they should be at work, but they don't recognize themselves in the description at all. When we have tried to do the values exercise, they haven't found any alignment between their perceived work self and their values. In fact, it's not uncommon to find that the perceived person is not someone they particularly like! How can we expect to be happy at work, if the person we are aspiring to be at work is someone who we wouldn't want to connect with?

Working with values makes our work, regardless of role, meaningful to us. Meaningful work is good for our mental health, and if we weave more of our values throughout our work, we will have more freedom, growth and opportunities. Work is meaningful when it aligns to our values.

Skills versus values

Be careful not to confuse your skills with your values as they are not the same. Our worth does not come from what we are good at or through particular skills that others admire. That is slice territory. Our values are what matters to us. Our skills may not align at all with our values or what we deeply care about. This is where making decisions about what we want to do, based purely on what we are good at, is not useful. For one thing, we know that what we are good at depends on many variables and changes and develops over time.

It is important to re-evaluate our values constantly and consider what matters to us now, in this moment, especially if we feel lost or disengaged at work. Some values will gather the strength of conviction over the years and will seem more important than ever. Others will decrease in importance to us. We have to allow ourselves the freedom to change, evolve, challenge and progress, and this includes in our work.

Get comfortable with being uncomfortable

Connecting to our values and sharing those with others means we cannot go wrong as our values are the very core of us. Authenticity is our superpower that helps connect us meaningfully both to our work and to those around us. As we'll see in the next two chapters, those who are around us are vital in building our HHSE, so it makes sense for them to get to know the real us.

Reworking authenticity

- Being authentic at work is a superpower we can use to boost our HHSE at work.
- Many of us recognize the importance of authenticity but struggle to bring our whole selves into the workplace.
- We are all whole cakes, no matter how much we want to be the perfect slice.
- Perfection is a social construct that doesn't objectively exist.
- Our values will always guide us back to our most authentic self.
- Being authentic will gain us true confidence and allow us to be HHSE at work.

10

Reworking Management

Who you work with matters. Those around us at work can directly boost or diminish our HHSE score. These next two chapters focus on understanding and reworking our team dynamics in order to truly work well.

In his book *Leadership Gold*, John Maxwell famously stated: 'People quit people, not companies.' This is often slightly misquoted to tell us that people leave managers not jobs. The role of a manager is crucial in supporting and promoting our happiness at work.

Teamwork starts with the team leader, and their management style can set the tone for the whole team. However, our management system is broken and is setting all of us up to fail.

Honestly, I have no idea why anyone would want to be a manager. The level of expectation appears ridiculous, and somewhere along the line we have lost sight of what it really means to be a manager, and who should be a manager in the first place. The system visibly fails time and time again and yet companies follow the same path. What was it that

Albert Einstein said? The very definition of insanity is doing the same thing over and over and expecting different results. Companies continue with the same management framework, and yet it doesn't support you, or your manager, to be well at work. In better understanding how and why our manager may not be able to be who we want them to be, or indeed why we cannot be the manager we strive to be, we can better engage with and protect our health and happiness at work.

Setting up managers to fail

As it stands, managers are rarely chosen for their management skills. Instead, the role of 'manager' is used as a path of promotion. Many individuals who become managers do so because there is no other way for them to progress within that company. These managers end up doing a role that they never asked for or claimed to be any good at. Can you imagine any other role in business being assigned this way? 'Our engineers aren't chosen for their engineering skills' or 'Our surgeons aren't chosen for their skill with a scalpel.' It simply wouldn't work.

Imagine a child playing in a sandbox. They are having a fantastic time playing and enjoying themselves, learning and developing, and they are excited to play in the sandbox every day. Then one day you tell them that they've done so well in the sandbox that now they get to stand outside the sandbox and watch everyone else play. Not only that, but they are now responsible for making sure all the other children play nicely, and that no one eats the sand (nor the random sticking plasters that lurk beneath the surface). Does that sound fun to you? Do you think that child would wake up excited to go to the playground every day? Even the children who might initially feel special and important will want to get back in there every now and then. This is what we do to managers. We hire employees to do a job they want to do and are excited about, and then, to reward them for being great at that job, we take them away from it. This is where it starts to go wrong.

There are, of course, some excellent managers. You may be one of them. They exist, and we see them within all different types of businesses. Managers who are supportive, kind and empathetic and who cheer you on as they see your career go from strength to strength. But, within the promotional management model, this is not a guarantee. Currently, your manager, and the support they offer you, is a complete lottery. Moreover, as business needs get tougher, managers are more likely to be hired for efficiency and delivery than for caring teamwork approaches. The company hiring you as a manager will have very different requirements of you than the employees you manage will. Your starting point is a huge discord between wants and needs, which immediately sets teams up for disappointment and sets managers up to fail.

Meet Simon

I hate being a manager. I always thought that, if ever I was a manager, I would be leading a team of likeminded individuals, working together to solve complicated technical issues. I envisaged a mini-gang, coming together to problem-solve and debate and work out new ways of working. When I got promoted to manager, I was told it was because I was a senior engineer and they wanted to progress me. I was pleased initially, thinking I could work with my team and come up with really innovative solutions, and earn a bit more money. On my second day as a manager, a colleague, and former peer, broke down in tears and told me they were getting divorced. I had no clue what to say. I've never been very good with stuff like that, so I just sort of awkwardly said I hoped they were OK. The next thing, there's a formal complaint against me because I didn't follow the protocol for compassionate leave or offer regular check-in meetings. I let them down, but I didn't mean to; I just had no clue what I was doing. I couldn't tell you the last time we had a brilliant discussion as a team. I have never felt further removed from my engineering work. I miss being a colleague and a peer. Being a manager is so hard.

Simon is a good person, but he isn't a good manager, which is fine because he never claimed to be. Simon is, however, an excellent engineer, so who thought it was a good idea to take him away from that role? Until companies get comfortable promoting people for their skillset without giving them additional management responsibilities, then we are all being set up to fail.

If ever you've struggled to connect with your manager, or found them disappointing or unsupportive, make sure you recognize this isn't about you. They aren't failing you; you are all being failed by a system that needs reworking and which makes management a lottery. This isn't your fault, but it isn't theirs either. No one accepts a role wanting to fail, and many managers feel as equally frustrated and disappointed as you do. This doesn't excuse poor management behaviour, but it does at least partially explain it.

It's not your manager's responsibility to manage your mental health

In almost every company I have worked with, employee wellbeing is handed to the managers to oversee. Companies spend an absolute fortune putting their managers through training to learn 'softer skills', a better name for which would be 'fundamental skills', as these are the core of what we need from our managers.

Managers are taught how to be better listeners, and how to understand and empathize with different people's viewpoints and life events. They also learn how to uncover their own unconscious biases, which is essential if we are ever to achieve equality in the workplace. However, managers receive this training on top of an enormous pile of other mandatory training. Often, this 'softer skill' training is optional, and so, given that a lot of progression and bonus options are dependent on mandatory training being completed, naturally that is what managers prioritize. Also, there is a self-selecting bias, with the managers who are already interested and engaged in these ideas tending to complete the training, while those who really need it, don't. Many companies take a 'sheep dip' approach to management training, running courses for all managers once or twice per year. This means that managers may receive training on how to be a manager when they are six to twelve months into the job already!

Wouldn't it make much more sense to hire managers who can showcase these existing skills? People managers with existing people skills, who coach, cheerlead, promote, engage with and support those they manage? That way, those wishing to be a manager could first complete the training and showcase their management talents.

Our managers are officially overwhelmed. Diversity and inclusion concerns? Speak to your manager. Submitting a flexible working request? Speak to your manager. Need a day off sick? Speak to your manager.

Thrown into the mix, alongside everything else, companies are training managers to be pseudo doctor–therapist hybrids, asking them to identify the symptoms of mental health issues in their team members. Of course, once you identify a problem, you need to act on it, and it is here so many managers are set up to fail. Mental health issue? Speak to your manager. But what does that actually mean? Why would an unqualified non-mental health practitioner be the best person to support your mental health? Your manager's role is to enable you to do your job. This means making sure you have the tools, skillset and equipment to do your role to the best of your ability. They don't know how to support each individual team member's mental health. They can put overall good HHSE practices in place, but you are ultimately in charge of your wellbeing.

Managers cannot be responsible for our mental health, and to hand that responsibility over to our managers completely disempowers us. We are the experts in our own lived experience, and only we can take control and make changes in our lives that will support our wellbeing. Our health and happiness are so fundamental – why would we risk delegating that to a manager who wasn't selected for those skills in the first place? We have to take accountability for our own health and wellbeing at work.

The 'do no harm' principle applies here. Your manager should not actively engage in behaviours that harm your health at work, including your mental health. Managers need to work with us and ensure they are not blocking our path by being obstructive in our development. However, they are *not* responsible for your wellbeing. That lies firmly in your own hands.

As the health and wellbeing at work conversation continues, more and more is being piled onto managers. This disregards the various medico-legal complications and the very varied personality and management styles, all of which influence how and when we might speak to our manager about our wellbeing.

It sounds cold, but we need to stop blaming our managers. They are there fundamentally to enable us to do our role. That's it. Handing over all responsibility for our health and wellbeing is not sustainable and sets everyone up for disappointment. The manager will feel they have failed, and you will feel failed by them. I'm not trying to excuse poor management but instead empower all of us to take back some control.

I hasten to add, I am not talking about bullying managers here. Bullying breaks the 'do no harm' rule and is a separate issue. There is no excuse for any form of bullying or harassment anywhere, but especially in the workplace where we should be safe, and employees need to take direct action if they are being bullied. All companies should have an anti-bullying and harassment policy, and all employees should be protected. No one should ever be made to tolerate bullying behaviour.

Bullying aside, if it is a personality clash, a struggle to progress, or a simple lack of support, then take a breath. It's not personal. It's something that needs reworking. Your manager probably wasn't hired to be a great manager of people but of workload. It's not an excuse, but it is a reason. This is why more than ever, we have to take control of our HHSE score. It is too important to delegate out to someone underqualified, overworked, and drowning in policy and paperwork. If you need to rework a difficult relationship with your manager, then here are three steps you can follow.

Dealing with a difficult manager

- **Speak to them.** Many people who struggle with their managers never speak to them about it. It doesn't need to be a big confrontation, but you do need to have a conversation if you are struggling. Gather some concrete examples of their behaviour or attitude that you feel is unsupportive and discuss with them what you would like to change. If your manager is very difficult and you struggle to work with them, then raise the issue, but don't blame them. Saying 'I've noticed a disconnect and would like a better working relationship with you' gives an opportunity for improvement. Saying 'You're a nightmare to work with!' doesn't. Try to raise this as soon as you can. Problems will become worse if left to fester unresolved. Raising issues like this prevents resentment building and helps to avoid uncomfortable conflict.

- **Don't be passive.** Managers won't always spot opportunities for you. Even the great ones are going to miss things, so you need to be active in your own development and support. If you can take a clear ask or question to your manager, you are far more likely to get a positive response. For example, rather than saying 'You haven't developed me', put in a request for a training course or ask to be involved in a particular project. Look outside your team and shadow a colleague in a different part of the business to gain different experiences. This is you being active and engaged in your work and empowers you so much more than waiting for your manager to develop you, and resenting it when they don't.

- **Put in the work.** Like any relationship, it takes both parties to be involved. What effort can you put into the relationship with your manager? What can you ask of them? What can you offer them? Seeing your relationship as a dynamic and developing entity allows you to regularly review and rework it.

Almost all of the cases I get pulled into which involve management disputes are due to a lack of understanding and communication. Once all sides are speaking, we are able to resolve the challenges which are causing deep unhappiness on both sides. A 'them and us' attitude towards management serves no one. We are all humans, working for the same company, doing our best in a broken system. Remember, it's not personal. It just needs reworking.

Reworking management

- Your manager may have been selected as a path of promotion, not for their management skills.
- Many managers are left without adequate training, resource or support and so are feeling their way through the role.
- Taking control and being proactive is the best way to engage with your manager.
- If something about your relationship with your manager is wrong, it's not personal.
- Communication, as early as possible, is key.

11

Reworking Teamwork

Almost all of us will work with other people. Whatever the size of the organization we work for, or even if we work for ourselves, we will connect, communicate and engage with others. The team around us can determine everything, from how much we enjoy work and value the company, through to how productive we are. Other people are too important to ignore, and if things aren't working, they need reworking.

Gallup, the global analytics firm which gathers data from the workplace around the world, poses an interesting question in its annual survey: 'Do you have a best friend at work?' Many people still draw a line between home and work and therefore consider their best friend to be in their home sphere, possibly from school or the neighbourhood where they grew up. However, Gallup is asking specifically about the workplace and places the emphasis on 'best' friend because it recognizes the impact of a meaningful and close relationship at work. So, do you have a best friend at work?

Friendships at work used to be frowned upon. Even today some old-school managers don't want people being too friendly at work as they view it as disruptive and counterproductive. They believe people will be too busy having fun and socializing to get the work done. Those managers are wrong. People who have a 'best friend' at work are shown to be happier and healthier in the workplace and are also seven times more likely to be engaged in their role.[1] Not only that, close friendships between employees boost productivity, retention and job satisfaction.

Those we work with have the ability to make us feel safe, motivated, connected and purposeful. However, they also have the power to disengage us and make us miserable, especially if team dynamics aren't working or if we feel constantly at loggerheads with our co-workers.

A strange situation

The idea of a team and team dynamics is a strange one. Within a team, we have a combination of many different people, with different ideas and personalities, all coming together to achieve the same goal. We get thrown together into the mix, under the heading of 'team', and are expected to work well together. Like all successful relationships, a healthy team dynamic is going to take work and dedication.

We don't get to choose our colleagues. In any other realm of our lives, if we were spending hours and hours together, we would think carefully about who we spend that time with. Imagine you had to go on holiday with a friend from your social circle. You wouldn't leave that to chance. You would think carefully about who you wanted to spend the time with, who is likely to want the same type of vacation as you, and whose company you would enjoy the most. All of that is just for one holiday together, whereas we spend a third of our entire lives at work. Our colleagues really matter.

Don't panic if your team isn't working, both literally and figuratively. If your team isn't being productive and engaging in their work, or if they are not getting on together and you're struggling to find your place in the team, then don't panic. Teamwork can be reworked and made a lot more comfortable. We're going to look at how teams form and work well, how to deal with toxic team members, and how to address unconscious biases that may be working against us. There are many ways that teamwork can be reworked. Let's start with the forming of a team.

There is a very normal team process which the American psychologist Bruce Tuckman identified in 1965: the 'forming, storming, norming and performing' process.[2] The forming and storming stages are typically where people may feel apprehension and see problems. Forming is your team coming together, and this is a constantly developing process as people join and leave a team, or team dynamics change (e.g. when a change in leadership occurs). When we are forming our teams, we are trying to figure things out, work out who is who, and trying to identify a role or 'fit' within the team. This can take quite some time, so if you are in a team and you feel you haven't found your place yet, then don't give up – it will happen.

The storming stage is the one people find very challenging, and often panic about, but it is a normal part of teamwork and needs to be approached calmly. It is the storm before the calm where the team falls into norming, where they are working well and performing, where they can achieve excellence. Storming is the stage where all the different characteristics, ways of working, opinions and beliefs come to the surface and can clash with one another. Naturally, this can lead to some challenging conversations, and people can experience friction and conflict.

The best way to manage this phase is to identify it, name it, and work together to move past it. Most people have heard of the Tuckman model, and storming, but some believe it happens on day one of a new team and then we all get past it and move on. But teams constantly storm. That's OK, and it's a normal part of team dynamics. Every new project or focus may lead to a storming phase as people challenge one another on the best way to do things or the roles each team member should take.

By highlighting the normality of the storming stage, you can prevent it feeling personal and help your team to recognize it as a healthy part of team development. Clear identity of roles and responsibilities will help people through the storming phase, as it alleviates anxiety and gives a clear focus. Leave storming unchecked and you'll find the team splits into different micro-teams based on similarity of thought and behaviours. This can lead to a rupture in the team which is hard to repair. Much like a split sauce, you cannot just leave it and hope it comes back together; it needs help. Revisiting roles, responsibilities, overall aims and the motivation for completion is a great way to reunite a split team and remind them of their joint purpose and the roles everyone has in achieving it.

HHSE boost: Reflection

- Has your team formed and stormed?
- Are you happy with the role you hold in your team or does it need reworking?
- What small step could you take today to rework your role in the team and boost your HHSE score?

A storming phase is a really positive opportunity to grow and build psychological safety into the team. We can ask ourselves, 'Are other people wrong or just different in their way of thinking?' As we know, when we are uncertain, we tend to stick with what we know, and so we may side with people with similar thinking and ideas. This isn't great for creative problem-solving or diversity as you will get the same ideas echoed back to you. Next time you feel your team is storming, deliberately seek out alternative views, work with people in the team you haven't typically connected with. Name where you are, and tell people in your team if you are feeling a little lost or out of place. This creates the psychological safety to openly explore and discuss team dynamics and rework what's needed to lead to positive change.

HHSE boost: Who is around you at work?

Take a moment to consider who is around you at work. This could literally be who you sit or stand next to, but also who you connect with on a daily basis. Who are you on the phone to or jumping on Zoom calls with? Consider the people you interact with most during your working days and reflect on the following:

- Who is around you?
- What are their feelings/attitudes/behaviours at work?
- Are they mainly positive or negative? An optimist or a pessimist?
- Do they reflect who you want to be at work?
- Is there diversity within your group? Do you have lots of different backgrounds, ages and experiences around you?

- Are you getting a wide range of opinions and thought in your group, or does everyone have the same mindset?

- Do you have people at all levels of seniority around you?

- How do interactions with those around you leave you feeling?

Think about your HHSE score. Do those around you support and boost your health and happiness at work? Are you engaged in team dynamics that don't feel authentic to you? Do you feel safe, respected and emotionally connected? What do you need to change in your team interactions to make you happier?

Toxic team energy

Have you ever met that person at work who just seems to love being miserable? You know the type. When someone new joins and asks them how long they have worked there, they roll their eyes and say, 'Oh gosh, don't ask!' or 'I'll tell you how long … *too* long!' They seem to complain about everything – from the IT equipment to the expenses policy to the taste of the coffee. They almost never have anything positive to say about work, and they interrupt any positive conversation around them with their cynicism and negativity. Then you find out they've worked there for ten years. What on earth?!

You would do well to be cautious of these colleagues. At first, they appear harmless. It can be amusing to have a colleague who has a sardonic tone and a sarcastic comment to throw about, and you know you are in very safe hands if ever you need a good moan about the printer being jammed again.

However, beware these colleagues. They are heavy weights, anchors that want to pull you down and keep you on a level with them. The saying 'Misery loves company' could have been invented for these people. They are destined to be unhappy because they are too busy complaining about every single element of the workplace and their job to be anything else. They don't want to progress, and they don't want you to progress either.

These tend not to be dedicated employees. They won't work hard, although they are usually the ones telling everyone how busy they are, while disrupting those who are genuinely busy and trying to crack on. These colleagues will have a knack for getting out of almost everything. They will disrupt your day with a 'meeting' in the calendar, when actually it turns out they wanted a coffee and a non-work-related chat. They are super friendly until you point out that you should get back to your desk, or that your break is nearly over. They neither comprehend, nor support your work ethic, and they don't appreciate the light you shed on theirs.

This colleague is not a friend; they are a saboteur. They won't want to see you rise or do well because this raises uncomfortable questions for them. If you start bettering yourself, then they might have to consider why they aren't bettering themselves. They will tell you that you are lucky to have your success and never acknowledge the effort involved. Similarly, they will never take accountability for their own lack of progress. It will all be someone else's fault. Someone doesn't like them, they fell out with the hiring manager, they aren't being supported, and so on. It is easier for them to accredit you with luck than to admit to their own lack of effort.

It sounds childish but that's because this is an immature dynamic and it is an immature individual who acts in this way. Be very mindful of who is around you, who is influencing you, who is cheerleading and supporting you, and be equally mindful of who is not.

If you have a toxic team member, then you need to manage them carefully in order to protect yourself. You can rework this dynamic in several ways:

- **Ask them if they are OK.** Point out to them that you have noticed that they are often negative about work and want to check whether they are OK. This is not you offering to solve anything for them, but gently highlighting that you've noticed their negativity and are wondering what's at the root of it.

- **Explain the impact on you.** If this colleague starts a negative conversation and it's affecting you, then stop the conversation and ask to talk about something more positive. Explain the impact the conversation is having on you and why you want to stop the conversation. You can do this gently and with humour, perhaps changing the subject entirely. The important thing is to stop the negativity before it impacts you.

- **Don't engage in negative chat.** If a colleague has a genuine problem and wants to discuss a difficult situation with you, then that is very different and you can offer and signpost towards appropriate support as necessary. However, if someone wants to constantly moan about work, with no interest in changing or solving anything, then this is exhausting. Don't stay in the conversation. Excuse yourself and move away. Humans are behavioural creatures and sometimes we need to see behaviour change in order to make our own changes. If every time someone is being negative, you move away from the conversation, they will learn to curb the negative chat in order to stay chatting with you.

Meet Selina

There was a little group of us who always went to lunch together, and two of my colleagues would spend the entire time slagging off their managers and pretty much everything about the workplace. I was in the middle of launching a new initiative, and they immediately told me how it would fail and that I shouldn't bother. They knew nothing about it but had already dismissed it and I was upset and annoyed by their negativity. I told them that I needed to stay high-energy and positive about the project in order to keep going with it and that I didn't find their comments helpful. They apologized and we agreed a 'no work chat' policy for our lunch breaks. We ended up having loads more in common to talk about, other than work, and they had some really fun stories. They were negative people, so no matter what we talked about they erred on the downside, but I found it affected me less as it wasn't directly related to me or my work.

Reworking your role in your team

As the team forms, we can find ourselves put in a role that doesn't feel authentic to us. We may get labelled as 'the quiet one' or 'the organized one' and end up not being consulted or left to sort out the details because everyone believes that's the role we play. It can be very uncomfortable to be in the wrong role. Remember the impact of not being authentic in the workplace? It's that 'uncomfortable sweater' feeling all over again. Ideally, within a team, you want flexibility to stretch yourself and engage in many different aspects of the work, in order to heighten your HHSE score. Being given a role you don't like or that doesn't feel authentic to you can quickly disengage you from your work.

If you feel stuck in a role, then imagine you are a lily pad and your team is a pond (bear with me). Although you look still and secure, you can move around in the pond. Ponds are filled with water, not cement, meaning you can move around, change roles and shift dynamics – we're never as stuck as we may perceive. In moving, we may create small ripples or even big splashes, but ultimately the water will settle and everyone will fall into their new places in the pond.

This is true of any role in our lives, in and out of work. Even though roles in family dynamics or friendship groups can feel immovable, we always have an opportunity to move around and change our role. Start making small changes and get the ripples in motion to move you around the pond. See how a new dynamic within the team feels. Even very small changes, such as suggesting you help with a project or someone works alongside you for a period of time, or having different conversations, can cause a significant shift. Reworking our role in this way can make us more comfortable, happier and more engaged, as well as feel more authentic. Remember, you are always in a pond, and never in cement. You can shift away from toxicity and damaging team dynamics, without having to leave, simply by starting with small ripples.

Dealing with unconscious bias

Meet Simone

I've worked in male-dominated teams throughout my career. The men in my teams would definitely deny any unconscious bias, but it's there. It shows itself in little ways. If we arrive in a meeting room and there are no refreshments, they'll turn to me and say, 'Is there any tea?' as though

I should be popping the kettle on because I'm the woman. Also, if someone needs to take the minutes in a meeting, everyone will look at me expectantly because I'm the woman and they assume I should take on secretarial duties, despite being one of the more senior partners in the room. It's funny how they don't see it because it is so obvious to me.

If you are in a team dynamic similar to Simone's, then you need to name the bias as it is happening. The trouble with unconscious bias is in the name – people are not aware of it. There's a wonderful saying: 'If you ask a goldfish "How is the water?", they'll reply "What water?" because they don't realize they're in something they are completely surrounded by.'

Highlighting when biases occur through open and honest conversations is the only way to manage and eliminate them. But it doesn't need to be confrontational, quite the opposite. Simone won't get far if she starts accusing everyone in her team of being 'sexist pigs', but she can highlight that just because she is a woman doesn't mean she is responsible for taking care of everyone, and suggest a solution-focused approach such as taking equal turns to order refreshments or take minutes.

Facing up to these continued biases in the workplace can feel exhausting, but if we want to see change, then we have to challenge them. If we have challenged them and nothing changes, then this gives us recourse to remind people of the fact: 'We agreed that I am not responsible for that' or 'We agreed to share that work equally.' Battling unconscious bias is challenging, but we need to remember that people are blind to it and we need to challenge our own thinking. Do we hold attitudes towards others that are unfavourable? Do we put all people of a same group into the same category? If you find yourself thinking, 'Typical male response!' or 'Well, they would say that because they're management' or 'My team doesn't care about XYZ', then catch yourself and explore these. Are they factual statements or are they assumptions?

There is a big difference between bias and discrimination, and in many jurisdictions, including the UK and the USA, there are protected characteristics to prevent and protect against discrimination. Protected characteristics include, but are not limited to, sex, age, marital status, gender reassignment, pregnancy/maternity, race, disability, sexual orientation, religions and beliefs. If behaviour is deemed discriminatory, then there is legal recourse to address this.

Biases won't always be as obvious: sometimes we just get a feeling that we are being treated differently but we don't know why. Hierarchical practices within teams can sometimes engender this type of bias.

Meet Vanessa

I worked in a psychiatric ward, and the consultant psychiatrist there, Jeremy, was lovely but definitely saw us as 'lowly' and the other consultants as his peers. He introduced me to people as Vanessa instead of using my 'Dr' title, but would introduce all the other consultant psychiatrists with their full titles. I don't care about my title usually, but I do care about being 'othered'. It wasn't on purpose, but that wasn't the point. It was an in-built bias and it needed changing.

Jeremy would also delay meetings to allow for consultants to join, but wouldn't wait for the nurses and other staff to join and wouldn't welcome them into the meeting when they did join. It really upset me because either we're a team or we're not. We can't say some people are more important than others, and we only need some of us in a team meeting. I could see other members of the team getting really upset about it, and I got really fed up of it and started to take a bit more control. If we were all there and one of his consultant buddies wasn't, then I'd say to Jeremy, 'Right, shall we start then? The team is here.' I always said it smilingly and never in a confrontational way, but I did say it every time. Sometimes Jeremy would say, 'We'll just wait for X because he'll have something important to say', and so I'd do the same about the nurses and occupational therapists and make a point of including them in the meeting and getting their updates. After all, they were the ones actually working with the patients day-in, day-out! Gradually, the team meetings only started when everyone from the team was present, and everyone contributed more and felt more valued. I also had a quiet word with Jeremy about the 'Dr' thing and he changed it immediately. These were small shifts but made a huge difference to how I felt about Jeremy and us working together.

Hierarchical practices are often inherited and accepted without challenge, on the basis that they pre-date any current members of staff. It is important that we highlight these and aren't afraid to challenge them. Although people may be more senior to us, they are still just people, and most want to do their best to be fair and decent colleagues.

Be a sponsor, not a mentor, within your team

Amber Hikes, Chief Equality and Inclusions Officer at the American Civil Liberties Union, shares a fantastic strategy for supporting others in the workplace to overcome biases and that is to aim for sponsorship, not mentorship. In an inspirational TED Talk, Hikes discusses how mentorship is advising others on how to make connections or telling them to speak up in meetings but sponsorship is actually making those connections and opportunities happen. Rather than saying to someone, 'Make sure your voice is heard in the meeting', it is inviting them to speak when you notice they are being ignored, or are not being asked their opinion. Sponsorship is a fantastic way to use your position, power and privilege to help someone over the line who would otherwise struggle to get there.

Imagine the teams we could have if we worked together, truly together, not othering managers or our teammates, and supporting positive team dynamics. When we take control, offer support and solutions and engage with our teams, we get so much out of them. We cannot change other people, but we can change how we interact with them to keep us happy, healthy, safe and engaged. We need to do the work to secure good relationships at work.

Reworking teamwork

- Have an internal locus of control. Take positive steps to support your own wellbeing at work and speak to others to align them with your goals.

- Be the positive change you want to see. If you want to be more positive at work then check the company you are keeping and the conversations you are having. Your vibe will attract your tribe, so the more positive you are in the workplace, the more positive your workplace will be.

- Challenge and take action. Don't resign yourself to behaviours or situations in work until you feel forced to literally resign. Instead, take proactive steps to support your wellbeing. Taking control is the ultimate way to empower your own HHSE and ensure your wellbeing at work remains strong.

12

Working Alone

Working alone is increasingly common. As hybrid working continues to grow in popularity, with UK employees, for example, spending only (a higher-than-average) 1.5 days per week in the office,[1] homeworking is a part of our typical working pattern. However, not every homeworker needs to be alone, and the idea of isolating ourselves and not seeing another human being for days on end needs reworking. There are plenty of steps that can be taken to keep us happy and healthy while we work from home. The trouble is, like many elements of work, no one has taught us *how* to work from home. We make many errors, from trying to replicate our day in the office at home (doomed to fail), to thinking we have to 'do it all' and never ask for help.

In writing this, I am mindful that not every job can be completed from home, and there are many jobs that can only be done on-site. However, we can all feel alone or isolated at work, and the tips in this chapter will support you if you *feel* you are solo working even in among a crowd.

The tips shared here will also help you with any other work that you need to get done at home, even if that's for personal projects as opposed to your paid work. Whether you need to do some admin or you finally want to have a crack at writing your debut novel, these tips will ensure you continue to work in a way that boosts your job satisfaction and overall HHSE score. Whether we work for ourselves, or work from home, or work in some degree of isolation, we need to rework how to work alone.

Lone working or lonely working?

Many roles within a company are one-deep, meaning you may be the only person that does your exact job. As has often been my experience, companies may hire you as a lone subject matter expert to ensure that they have a particular area covered, at least on paper. Even if you do work within a team, you may have no one to discuss your work with; instead, you simply report on progress. This type of team is not a team in the truest sense, as it doesn't provide you with a support system. Working in this way can leave you feeling lonely and isolated.

HHSE boost: Reflection

- Do you have a team?
- What does that team offer you?
- What is your role within the team?
- Consider what we have already learned about teams and team dynamics. Is there anything you would like to change about your team dynamic?
- If you work alone and don't have a team, then who is in your network?
- Who do you connect with?
- Who is around you day to day?

If you are a lone worker, and particularly if you work for yourself, then you need your network. You need regular interactions with positive influences who are supporting you and cheering you on. You don't need to do it alone. When you work for yourself, you adopt many different roles and it can feel lonely to have to be all things to all people. We need people to have informal conversations with, to chat with, to connect with. This day-to-day networking and connection will boost your HHSE score and is essential to workplace wellbeing.

The idea of having a coffee with a friend or a catch-up call during the working day can feel as though we are neglecting our work. However, social connection is crucial in the workplace. It leads to better engagement, customer relations, work quality and wellbeing and is linked to lower safety incidents. In other words, your network keeps you happy, healthy, safe and engaged. When we work alone, we have to put effort into and plan these interactions, as they won't happen informally, as they do, say, when bumping into someone in an office. It can feel somewhat awkward to suggest a catch-up or a coffee with someone when you are both 'supposed' to be working, but it's important to see these interactions as an integral part of your working day.

We grew up in school environments where we were told to sit quietly and get on with our work, and many of us carry that behaviour into adulthood. We tell ourselves, 'If I am working, then I should be sitting quietly.' But these environments don't always allow us to work well. Connecting with your network will keep you focused, allow you to decompress, share troubles, and prevent you stewing on something minor, turning it into a big deal in your own mind. Also, informal chats can help you problem-solve, think creatively and gain alternative perspectives. I'm sure you've had conversations with friends or colleagues where you accidentally solve a problem, or get a really helpful perspective, without asking for it. Organic and natural conversations can offer solutions that we didn't know we were looking for.

When we work for or by ourselves, we worry that we won't get our work done if we take time out for these interactions. Instead of worrying about the impact of having these interactions and connections, we should all be more concerned by the impact of not having these throughout our working day. We all benefit from connection, and we need to deliberately and mindfully plan our connections when we work alone.

Activity: Plan your connections

Go through your calendar right now: see where your moments of connection are and invite someone to connect with you for a catch-up. No agenda, just an informal interaction. Take time for this catch-up. Don't be half in the room and simultaneously checking your phone and thinking about what you 'should' be doing. If you work shifts or cannot step away from your work, then seek connection points within the workplace. Is there a coffee break where you can catch up with others? Can you chat with someone while walking around a site visit? However you can do it, do it. Fully immerse yourself in the experience of that connection.

How did it feel? What did/didn't you like about the catch-up? Was it the right time? The right length? The right person? Did you feel uplifted by the conversations you had? Did it leave you feeling happier, healthier, safer and more engaged in your work?

Continue to build interactions into your working day and pay attention to how you feel at the end of each one. Do this regularly and suss out what works best for you and make sure it's a regular practice. Doing so will keep you from lonely working, even if you work alone.

You and your workspace – panic stations

For many of us, lockdown was the first time we had experienced working from home for any extensive period and there was little to no time to consider where we could work well. We set up our workstations in a panic, not giving a thought to how we wanted to work, where we wanted to work, and what would support our health and happiness longer term.

This was understandable at the time as it was hugely discombobulating and we just needed to make something work, and quickly. It's fair to say these emergency workstations were not ideal. You may have set up on your ironing board, or worked from your bedroom, sofa or garage. You may even have resorted to working from the toilet, either for a bit of respite from the kids, or because that's where the WiFi was strongest! Whatever the reason, we found ourselves working in less than ideal set-ups. What astonishes me is how many people continue to work from their panic stations. We cannot continue to work from a place of crisis ad infinitum and we need to reflect on what works and what doesn't work.

The next chapter will show you how to rework your space for ultimate cognitive wellness and how to set yourself up with a brilliant HHSE-boosting workspace. This chapter is asking you to reflect and consider your current homeworking practices, and whether they are keeping you happy, healthy, safe and engaged.

HHSE boost: Reflection

Take a moment to consider where you work. How do you feel when you walk into your workspace? Do you feel energized, focused and as though you are slipping into 'work mode'?

If you are nearby as you read this, then walk into your workspace and pay attention to how you feel. If you are not nearby, then go there in your mind. Do you feel any resistance to going to your workspace? As you stand there ask yourself: what is my body doing? Is there tension anywhere? Is my jaw clenched or relaxed? How am I standing?

Then consider the following:

- What emotions does your workspace evoke for you?
- Are you productive in that space?
- Do you enjoy spending time in that space?
- What would you want to do to improve that space?

When the pandemic, and with it the mandate to work from home wherever possible, started, I was in a meeting room and an executive director was asked where people could work. They replied, in a flustered tone, 'Well, wherever you can work, work there.' I interrupted and said, 'If I may rephrase that: wherever you can work well, work there.' Changing their sentence by just one word brought wellbeing back into the centre of work. This wasn't just about creating a space to sit with a laptop, but about creating a space for working well.

Flicking the switch

Working from home brings with it many advantages and perks, not least saying goodbye to hellish rush-hour commutes. But what we gain in time, we lose in the ability to separate work from home. How easy are you finding it to switch off after work? A clear distinction between work and home is essential to our wellbeing, and being in different locations does help us disconnect after a working day, so we need to know how to switch from work to home.

If home used to be the place we escaped to after a long day at work, where do we escape to now? Can we really feel that same sense of joy at 'coming home' just from shutting down the laptop?

It can be a real struggle to switch off from work and slip into 'home mode'. When we work in the same area we relax in, it becomes even more challenging to resist the pull of work. Just one more email? A quick glimpse at the inbox while dinner is cooking? A cheeky message on the work WhatsApp group? It all adds up, and before we know it work is creeping into all our precious spare time and we end the day feeling overwhelmed.

Below are five key tips to help you flick the switch from work to home and back again so that you can enter the 'zone' when you need to work and step out when it's home time.

1 **Have distinct work hours.** You might not like the rigidity of a schedule but your brain loves it. Our brains want certainty and structure. If you have set hours during your day that you dedicate to work, your brain will be primed to

work and you will feel more motivated and focused during these hours. Without a schedule you may feel listless and disengaged because all your brain is seeing is endless time stretching ahead. Pick a set number of hours that work for you and stick with them. Remember your energy peaks and dips. Your working hours need to be realistic and capture your natural motivation and creativity peaks as well as times when you are least likely to be disturbed.

2 **Have a start and finish ritual.** Running through the same routine at the start of work tunes us into the fact that we are about to begin working, and again, our brain values the prompt. Equally when we finish work for the day, we want a shut-down ritual and ideally want to pack every work-related item away and move it out of sight. Although it can feel a bit cumbersome to pack away our keyboard, laptop, phone, notebook and so forth every evening when we will be using them again the following morning, in reality it takes less than two minutes and is a really important signal to our brains that the work day has ended. It also creates just enough friction in the process that we won't easily be tempted to 'just quickly log on'.

3 **Dress for work.** You may not need the full suit but you definitely shouldn't be working in your pyjamas. You want your relaxation clothes to be for exactly that, relaxing. Clothes are a valuable cue to your brain that you are/are not working, and it's unfair to expect your brain to provide you with flashes of inspiration if you are wearing the clothes it associates with sleep and rest. Conversely, can we really expect to relax and sleep well in the clothes we have taken difficult calls and meetings in? Have your wardrobe divided into work and home clothes and consider your work 'uniform' a tool for motivation and your comfies the perfect kickstart for relaxation.

4 **Make relaxation look different.** If we stare at a screen all day for work and then walk into the next room and watch the TV, our brains don't realize that we are no longer at work. To be fair to our brain, even if we are half watching TV and half scrolling Instagram, then all our brain knows is that we are looking at a screen and looking at our phone which, to our brain, looks like working. This makes it hard to relax, and thoughts from our working day will continue to whirl around our minds as we haven't switched into relaxation mode. Doing something completely different immediately after work is key to letting our brains know it's home time. It can be anything: cooking a meal, walking the dog, taking a shower ... Any activity that doesn't mirror a work activity is a great introduction to your 'home zone'.

5 **Structure your work time.** This isn't just about working hours but also our patterns of self-care. If our brain knows that at certain hours of the day we will eat, relax, walk, read and go to sleep, then it will accommodate those activities. When days are very unstructured, then that uncertainty can generate some low-level anxiety which will leave us more prone to stress and agitation, both at work and at home. This doesn't mean we can't be spontaneous and build fun into our week, but we need some sort of structure so that our brains can support us with optimal functioning for both work and home activities.

Using physical cues is the best way to support our brains to make the mental switch from work mode into home mode and back again. These simple tools support us to have great routines, better mood, motivation and focus, better concentration, and, most importantly, an increased ability to rest and relax when we are not working.

The eight hours myth

Let's review our working day. The eight-hour day was established in a different century, for different purposes and with very different jobs in mind than those most of us do today. Yet it is a working pattern that many of us are stuck with.

One of the biggest objections continually levied at homeworking is a feared lack of productivity. There is a perception that a full eight-hour working day can only be achieved in an office, as homeworking is full of distractions that stop us focusing. This is a myth.

Your average office worker is productive for less than three hours per day.[2] Your average factory worker can only maintain full-throttle concentration and productivity for four hours per day maximum. Homeworkers, by contrast, have been shown to be 60 per cent more productive than office workers. But let's be realistic. The idea that we can maintain and have even levels of productivity for a full eight hours is nonsense. Human beings fluctuate. Everything from energy, hormones and motivation will constantly shift throughout the day. Why do we continue to hold ourselves to and perpetuate a way of working that simply isn't feasible? Our view of productivity needs reworking.

Once we accept that we cannot be productive for the entire working day, we can alleviate guilt. So many homeworkers work longer hours, due to the pressure they put themselves under to be productive. Also, homeworkers tend to dedicate their 'extra' time – for example time when they are not commuting – to work. Imagine that. You are gifted an extra one to two hours in your day, and you immediately hand them over to work. What if you kept those hours back? Just because you used to sacrifice it to travel, an extra hour in your day is not to be thrown away. If you were stuck in traffic, or packed onto an underground train, then you wouldn't be able to work. So why are you trying to work the extra time?

We may choose an early start because we enjoy the uninterrupted time first thing, before everyone else hops online or gets into the office. But is it really a choice?

Meet Casey

I'm a morning person, and I used to love the quiet time ahead of a busy working day where I could just crack on. However, I hit some problems. People became aware that I was working from around 7 a.m. onwards, and instead of it being my choice to work a couple of extra hours, it became an expectation others had of me. I would get emails from people asking me to prepare things for 9 a.m., which was technically the time my working day started. I'd get people asking me to cover their early meetings and calls because 'you're in anyway'. When I started working from home, people would call me from 6 a.m. onwards, and be quite stroppy if I didn't answer. It meant that my working day had moved from eight hours to over ten hours, without me agreeing, and with no extra pay or compensation in sight. It was no longer my quiet catch-up time, but was actually just work time, and I felt as though I needed to apologize if I wasn't available. I had no time for me at all. I wasn't having breakfast, I wasn't going for a morning run, I wasn't doing anything for me. I was quickly exhausted but had no idea how to get out of the hole I'd dug for myself. I actually considered leaving in order to start afresh with new routines.

When we work from home, we have to rework our working day and take back control. In fact, the biggest opportunity that comes with homeworking is the ability to have more control over how we spend our time. But you must create and maintain firm boundaries with yourself and with others (including whoever else is at home) in order to ensure that you are shaping your day. If you don't control your day, then someone else will.

Working for yourself

Whether you work for yourself, or by yourself, you need to start your working day by doing the work for you. By this, I mean prioritizing yourself at the beginning of the day, purposefully, mindfully and with your health and happiness in mind. Work for you means doing the activities that matter the most to you, before you leap straight into work. Your working day can support your wider health and wellness once you build in the work for *you* first.

Meet Laurel

I used to hate my mornings. I'd check my emails first thing, and I would always get pulled into something or someone would have put a call in immediately. Often, I'd be sat there in my dressing gown on the phone for over an hour. I remember the postman coming once at 10 a.m. and laughingly saying 'Nice to have a lie-in!' and I wanted to throttle him because I'd actually been working since 6.30 a.m. and hadn't had a break to shower or get dressed! I was always rushing and starting my day super stressed out. Also, I would be rushing the kids like mad, shouting at them to get ready, because I needed to get them to school and then I needed to dash back for early meetings. I'd spend the day with epic levels of mum-guilt. I was miserable. The kids were miserable, and mornings were rushed and chaotic. The more I worked, the more work I had to do. I never felt on top of anything, no matter how many hours I put in.

Laurel, like many of us, had lost sight of herself. Her mornings didn't feature her at all. They were all about others. Emails, other people's demands and her children took over. What she needed was buried underneath what everyone else needed.

On reviewing the situation, Laurel saw that she was giving work an additional three hours every day, at the cost to her, and her children's, happiness. Laurel reworked her day and began to put in boundaries and good working practices to support her wellbeing.

Laurel started by reiterating her working day. At the bottom of her email signature, she stated her working hours, and she blocked out her diary before 9 a.m. every day so no one could put in meetings. Laurel really wanted to start her day calmly, and so she found a 'wake-up' yoga meditation that was suitable for kids and she and her children did it together in the mornings. Sometimes the kids weren't up for it, but that was OK – Laurel made it a part of her morning routine regardless and the kids knew that this was 'Mummy's waking-up time'. Laurel made her mornings about her and her children, ahead of reading any emails. This was a game changer.

It was such a simple change but I felt as though I gained a whole extra day, which I guess I did across the week. The kids knew that the yoga helped Mummy wake up, and my youngest used to come in and sometimes just watch me. One day he said, 'Mummy, you smile more now,' which, ironically, made me cry (!) but [they were] happy tears. I didn't want my kids starting their day with me shouting at them. Also, I felt better for dropping them off when we were all in a good mood. Not every day goes smoothly, but I handle the rubbish mornings better because I'm just not as stressed. No one at work pushed back against me not being available. To be honest, no one really noticed. I was all wound up and defensive to begin with, ready with my answers should anyone question me. But, of course, no one did. All that stress and pressure was in my head. Once I gave myself permission, I could not only do it, but it was easy. I just had to rework my day, putting me first.

Taking time to plan the work you do for yourself, ahead of anyone else, is vital to staying happy, healthy, safe and engaged in your work. Sometimes, we can feel lost without the rhythms and pull of others directing our day. On the surface it is easier to be a passenger and just go with the ride, but in doing so we often end up somewhere we don't want to be. By putting in the work for yourself, before anyone else, you can change your whole working day, and live with more purpose and presence.

So how do you work for yourself first?

1 **Write your to-do list *before* checking your emails.** Writing your to-do list ahead of reading anyone else's demands of you will make sure that you are prioritizing what you need to get done. Sometimes we are so used to filling our day by responding to other people's needs that we struggle to write our own list. If this is you, then write down activities and tasks that focus on you, your health and wellbeing. This will ensure you prioritize yourself first within your working day.

2 **Do your thing first.** Whatever it is that you want to do, get it done *before* you start your working day. Want to work out? Meditate? Spend time with your kids? Start writing your novel? Whatever it may be, getting it done *before* work means that you are letting yourself and your brain know

that YOU are your priority. When we sacrifice everything for work, we get stuck in that mindset. When we do our own things first, then we are sending ourselves a message that we are important.

3 **Tune into what you need.** It's important to have some flexibility in your self-work. You may plan to do a workout, but not sleep well the night before and need to rest. Don't turn your self-work into another punishing routine. Instead, tune into what you want to achieve and have flexibility so that you can prioritize your health and wellbeing.

4 **Let others know your plans.** Let others know that you are not available. You don't need to justify your plans to anyone, but letting others know that you are putting yourself first allows for some gentle accountability, and some much-needed support, while you focus on you.

5 **Make sure you are on your to-do list.** So often we prioritize others. If you have kids to take to school, dogs to walk, parents to check in on or others who rely on you, then you can confuse your time with their time. If you have others who need your time, then it is even more important that you have time just for you built into your working day. Even if it is a regular coffee break, where you get to sit and do nothing but look out of the window, then put it in your calendar. You deserve and need time for you. Make sure time for you is built into your working day, every day.

Reworking solo power

Working alone requires a good understanding of our energy, motivation and when we are at our most creative. We need to understand our solo power, how we can best work with it, and how to ride the natural fluctuations in our energy and mood throughout the working day.

I'll bet you've had a day, probably when you were really busy, where you haven't got a thing done, because you spent the whole day procrastinating. It's the worst. However, if you went down a shame-spiral, telling yourself that it's because you are lazy or incapable, then you need to know that it simply isn't true. We all need to better understand what powers us, and depletes us, in order to work well alone and overcome procrastination.

Power down

Procrastination is the (seemingly) voluntary and irrational delay of an intended course of action – for example completing a task.[3] We can be really hard on ourselves when we procrastinate. You know the feeling: you have a to-do list as long as your arm, you have loads of projects to get on with … and you just … don't. You find yourself avoiding the work, or doing literally anything but (sudden urge to tidy the sock drawer anyone?). We often blame and berate ourselves for not being productive and getting on with it, but procrastination is not laziness. There are many reasons why we procrastinate, especially when working alone and are not being held accountable by an 'audience' of colleagues. We need to rework our criticism and focus on why we are really procrastinating, in order to overcome it.

1 **We're not dealing with uncomfortable emotions.**
   We procrastinate as a way to avoid uncomfortable emotions we feel about a task, such as overwhelm, fear and anxiety. When we feel overwhelmed by a task, we ignore it, hoping it will go away and we won't have to deal with it, even if we rationally know that won't happen. We can't blame ourselves for wanting to avoid uncomfortable emotions, but we do need to overcome them. Recognizing what we are avoiding is the first step in dealing with them, allowing us to

re-engage in our task. Have you ever not completed something for your boss? You avoid it for as long as you can and then avoid it further so as not to deal with the anxiety and guilt. Then the 'urgent' emails start arriving. You feel even more overwhelmed. Your boss puts in a meeting to discuss it. Urgh. The longer we avoid uncomfortable emotions, the more we let them thrive. Face the task. Face the emotions. Get it done. Move on. Avoidance makes discomfort worse and depletes our power. Facing things head-on is the only way to take back control.

2 **We don't reward success.** Humans are behavioural beings and we are motivated by reward. If we complete a task and get a reward, our brain will motivate us to do another one, in order to get another reward. So far, so simple. Except, often we forget about the reward part. We go from task to task and completely forget to stop and reward ourselves and celebrate the small wins along the way. As we move from one project or task to another, we use up our reserves of willpower and motivation and they slowly run out. We forgot to top them up with a reward. Why would we write the next report when we seemingly had no reward for writing the last one? We have to reward our own success.

Pro tip

Unless our reward is immediate, our brain will discount it. We cannot say to ourselves, 'Once I've done this task, I'll stop and have a nice cup of tea,' and instead quickly check our emails, take a phone call and answer a Teams query, because, by the time you get that cup of tea, your brain has lost all connection between the initial task and the reward. If you are feeling motivated, then one reward at the end of the working day may be enough, but if you are struggling to get going, then you need to be thinking about rewards for every task completed, no matter how small.

3 **We don't know what we are doing.** If our ultimate aim or goal is too abstract, then we won't know where to begin and we will continue to put something off. Take a goal such as 'get fit'. This is very vague and doesn't give us any clear direction on what we need to be doing. Whereas if you have a goal of 'do 20 minutes of walking at lunchtime today' then suddenly you have a much clearer and more motivating goal. Knowing exactly what we are doing, and how we are going to do it, stops us pushing it to the bottom of the to-do list and helps us get it done. Take a look at your task list and decipher what is involved in each task and write it out in specific steps. This will help you wriggle out of procrastination and into productivity – just don't forget to reward yourself.

4 **It's too far in the future.** We put off what is in the future, often needing an imminent deadline before we begin. We covered how some of our dopamine receptor activation and our unnatural triggering of our stress response is preventing us from starting something until the deadline is uncomfortably close. This may be the root of the 'present bias' people show when they choose to engage in activities that will reward them in the short term at the expense of those goals that would have better outcomes for the future.[4] We need to break our tasks into short-term wins that we can reward in order to stay motivated.

5 **We don't know when our energy peaks and dips.**
Understanding when our energy peaks and dips means we
can plan accordingly. This is at the root of utilizing your
solo power. Try monitoring your activities for a week and
noting how you feel during each one.

Understanding when and why we work best lets us harness
our solo power. We can build our activities into the times we
know we will be at our best. We can schedule effortful tasks
when we feel energized and motivated, and less cognitive
tasks when our energy is lower or we know we can't get into
deep work. Getting to know ourselves as a solo worker, and
knowing what works best for us, will allow us to stay happy,
healthy, safe and engaged, and keep us working alone, well.

Reworking working alone

- Connection and network are vital to boost our wellbeing
  when we work alone.
- Our workspace needs to allow us to work well, not just
  be wherever we can fit our laptop.
- The eight-hour working day is outdated and was
  designed for reasons and roles that are not applicable
  to the type of work we do today. We cannot be
  productive for eight solid hours.
- You need to do the work for yourself before you start
  your working day. You are your number-one priority.
- Procrastination is not laziness but a protective coping
  mechanism to help us deal with big emotions or
  uncertainty. We can break tasks down, reward
  ourselves and monitor our reactions to tasks to
  overcome our own blockers and remain HHSE in our
  working day.

13

Reworking Our Workspace

Don't you love walking in somewhere and instantly warming to the vibe? You can't put your finger on it, but there's something about the design, the feel, the atmosphere that just works for you. You feel instantly at ease and comfortable, or uplifted and excited to be there. You can also experience the complete opposite where you walk into somewhere and hate it. Something feels off, the lighting is wrong or it feels unfriendly. The environment we walk into evokes different moods and feelings in us and where we work is no different. The previous chapters have looked at how we work, this chapter focuses on where we work.

Why our workspace matters

Our workspace is one of the most influential factors on our mood day-to-day and affects how happy, healthy, safe and engaged we are. But we tend to tune out of our working environment. We become so used to our surroundings that we almost stop seeing them, only paying attention when a problem arises. The busier we get, the worse those problems will need to be in order to grab our attention. Imagine that. We only pay attention to that which is damaged, broken or irritating or that which has stopped serving us. This is not the way to engage with our workspace.

When we go to work for someone else, we are joining their premises, their set-up, their preferences. Very few of us will have our own private office where we choose the décor and hang our favourite art on the walls. Similarly, workstations tend to be built around working machinery and the necessary order of parts, rather than the individual operator, especially if they are shared spaces. When we work in an environment over which we feel we have no control, we can struggle to feel a sense of connection and belonging. We force ourselves to adapt to the working environment, rather than adopt a way of working that suits us.

The environment we find ourselves in affects everything from our mood, our motivation and our ability to concentrate, right the way through to our ability to breathe easily, and even who we might marry! Knowing the workplace is so important to our personal safety – our engagement in our work, our health and our happiness means we need to know where it's going wrong, so that it can be reworked.

Open-plan offices – the common enemy

Prior to the pandemic, 70 per cent of office workers worked in an open-plan office.[1] The principles of an open-plan office are simple. Everyone works on the same floor and in the same space, with no cubicles or walls separating them. Open-plan offices are supposed to encourage collaboration and equality, highlighting, as they do, a lack of ego from managers who leave their glass walls behind to come and sit among the team.

The idea of removing all barriers and walls between people was to encourage greater communication and reduce email traffic. However, without any noise absorption, many of us are too inhibited to chat in an open-plan office, as we are all too mindful of the lack of privacy and the potential to disturb others. This means, far from being a collaborative space, open-plan offices lead to awkward silence and overuse of instant messaging services. Many an eye roll is delivered when our inbox pings with an email from someone sitting three seats behind us, but in reality, they may have been too afraid of disturbing us, and those around us, to initiate an actual conversation. Far from enabling open conversation and collaboration, open-plan office layouts silence us.

The lack of privacy in offices also poses a real challenge. Having a beauty salon call to check which waxing treatment I was booked in for after work was particularly painful to navigate while sitting within earshot of my boss. Walking around with our mobile clamped under our chin saying, 'Sorry about this – I'll just find a room I can talk in', can make life feel a lot more stressful and complicated than it needs to be.

A study of employees in a simulated office environment for just eight minutes found that open-plan office noise heightened negative mood by 25 per cent.[2] Even such a short exposure showed an increase in negative mood and sweat response, an indicator of increased stress. If that's the impact of eight minutes then imagine what eight hours could do to your mood! The study was not designed to be especially aggravating. The simulated noise consisted of printer noise, phones ringing, people speaking at reasonable volume and so on – in other words, all the background noise that we can expect to encounter in a typical office and which many of us will be familiar with.

I can't work at work

People often opt to work from home, or outside the office space, in order to concentrate. In other words, we need to get away from the office in order to be more effective at doing our work. Surely that cannot be conducive to fostering engagement and satisfaction in the workplace?

Meet Callum

When I am on-site, I am in the office, and to be honest, I don't feel I do any actual work. I sit in back-to-back meetings and spend time with people face-to-face, which is wonderful and exhausting in equal measure. I don't often get a lot of actual work done. All the work and actions that come out of these meetings need to be done somewhere, but it's rarely at work. I say to my director, 'I come in to be social, I do the actual work at home.'

If this sounds familiar, then we need to be mindful of what our week looks like and the balance it offers us. Too much office and meeting time and no time to actually do the work that these meetings generate is not useful. However, we shouldn't have to choose between work and home in order to get work done. Ideally, we want a multitude of options that work well for us and that support the way we want to work. A well-designed workspace can offer them all and meet the varying individual needs we may have, dependent on project and personal demands and preferences.

I am a huge advocate of designing for cognitive wellness, and one of my biggest issues with open-plan offices is how all the space looks the same, which doesn't support how our brain works. These spaces require us to shift in and out of varying modes – meeting mode, social mode, lunch mode, deep-work mode … yet they offer us no physical cues to indicate any variation. The space where we share a cup of tea and a catch-up with a colleague is the same space where we have to get into some deep work, take a challenging meeting, problem-solve or try to bring a team together. We are expecting our brains to click into different modes without any physical prompts or changes in our environment. There are so many perks to being in the office, many of which are being lost in the stubborn refusal to redesign and re-energize office spaces, meaning more and more people are choosing to work from home. Why would you work from a space that doesn't suit you?

What about your HHSE score?

Poor workplace design can lead to a 25 per cent loss of job satisfaction and is linked to lower performance and higher stress. That office or workspace you walk into every day is affecting how happy and engaged you feel in your work. Not only that, but there are also direct impacts on our health and safety. Thirty-two per cent of workers reported that their workspace negatively affected their physical and mental health, with 36 per cent saying that they would be less likely to take sick days if their workplace was more inspiring.[3] If you are feeling low in mood, or are struggling to get motivated, a poorly designed workplace may be the root cause.

No one sets out to design an office that deliberately makes people unhappy and stressed. However, just one building is often trying to meet the individual needs and preferences of tens, if not hundreds, of people. It's a very tricky balance and one which is rarely well executed, simply because it is a near-impossible task. Some office designs showcase fantastic intentions, but in reality they simply don't work.

If we build it, they will ... sort themselves out

Meet Khenan

The office was designed with lots of different areas in mind but they weren't well thought through. For example, there was a dedicated quiet zone where you could go and work uninterrupted, but they put it right next to the little coffee/kitchenette area. This was a space where people naturally gathered and would be chatting and having informal catch-ups while they made a cup of tea, but they were constantly disrupting those who had deliberately sought out peace and quiet. This was more than poor planning; this heavily impacted employee wellbeing and so many people couldn't find the peace and quiet they needed. Even though the office was constantly busy and some areas were overcrowded, some areas were completely ignored and were a waste of space. We only had one large presentation space. It was right in the middle of a square office and there were banks of desks nearby. The trouble was no one could think straight because you were constantly competing to be heard. If you were in a presentation, then you couldn't hear because people would be nearby on calls or trying to have team meetings. Also, you couldn't plan anything quietly as a team because everyone could see and hear everything, so sometimes people would jump in or interrupt you with their suggestions. Often, people would walk through the middle of the area because they couldn't be bothered to walk around it, even if there was a meeting happening! It was as though they didn't respect the place at all, and people began to feel disrespected personally. On paper it was the perfect workspace because all these different areas existed, but no one had thought through the logistics of working there.

Creating a well-designed and high-functioning office space is an art form and should not be attempted without proper research and groundwork. If the spaces are available but the culture is not supportive of the design, then you end up with a lot of wasted space and a lot of frustrated employees. An office should be designed with, and for, the employees using it. Rather than blindly plonking employees into spaces, they should be introduced to the spaces, helped to understand the design and the thinking behind them, and asked to consider how they might use each of the spaces effectively. When we are involved in the design of a workspace, research shows that we are more likely to create meaningful change, positively impacting health and wellbeing across the organization.

HHSE boost

Consider your office space and work set-up:

- What can you influence?
- What can you add or remove to support your tasks?
- What can you rework to suit you better?

Better engagement in our workspace keeps us safer and healthier, not to mention happier due to the boost in connection. This is one way of engaging with work that we can all do, no matter what job we are in.

The politics of hot desking

Working as a consultant, my seating arrangements are often forgotten about until, on day one, I ask the question: 'So, where do you want me?' I'll then be met with a slight panic and usually some hastily squeezed-in seat will be found, upsetting the usual occupants and making me feel awkward and unwelcome. If you've ever seen the film *Late Night*, you'll have seen a new writer, played by Mindy Kaling, arriving in a TV studio for her new job and having to turn a trashcan upside down in order to create a seat. My experiences haven't been quite that extreme, but they haven't been far off.

Hot desking is often sold as the answer to workplace design issues. Hot desking offers the freedom for people to choose where they want to sit and has been shown to have some positive impacts. It should be noted though that much of the benefit serves the company, not us, with hot desking optimizing real-estate utilization and costs, saving companies a healthy 30 per cent.[4]

However, there are negatives to hot desking, and much like the open-plan office, it won't suit everyone. Research estimates that between 15 and 20 per cent of UK adults are neurodivergent and shows that the open and ever-changing work environment can feel especially chaotic and confusing for those with sensory challenges caused by bold patterns or harsh lighting.[5] Working in these surroundings radically impacts HHSE scores, as neurodivergent individuals report feeling unhappy and unsafe in their working environment. Given that neurodiversity runs on a spectrum, many of us would benefit from a calmer working environment, even if we don't identify as neurodivergent. The continued inability to form a set structure to the day, caused by open-plan and hot-desking environments, disengages us, making us feel out of place and as though we cannot connect with our workplace. There can also be the challenge of finding our fellow teammates, thus restricting collaboration and increasing email traffic. If we are uncertain where someone is sitting, and don't fancy walking around the office looking for them, then we are more likely to drop them a line, whereas a conversation may have provided an instant idea or resolution to a problem. It's an inefficient way of working, and also political, as Maria's testament shows.

Meet Maria

I know people who insist on sitting within a certain square footage of the CEO. Equally, I have known people not wanting to be associated with senior leaders and trying to sit as far away as possible. As much as people try to introduce and embed the notion of hot desking, humans are territorial creatures and it simply doesn't work for everyone. When I worked in central London, the company moved offices and introduced a hot-desking 'sit wherever you like' policy and it was chaotic. People openly admitted to leaving home 30 minutes earlier so that they could get in and bag 'their' desk. Many minutes were wasted if you fell victim to a delayed train and found yourself wandering around the entire office looking for a seat before setting up in the canteen or reception. I found this particularly demotivating. My commute took me roughly 90 minutes to two hours depending on how the trains were running. I took the first train that ran in the morning and so I physically couldn't get to work any earlier. I lost out in the game of musical chairs to those who had a ten-minute walk to work and could therefore get in early and nab their desk of choice. I resented going in and not having a desk to work at.

Choosing where you sit in an office has wider implications than mere preference. Where you sit determines who you network with, who you have access to, who sees you, your pathway to promotion and even who you may marry! One in ten couples meet their significant other in the workplace, and so where you sit and who you connect with could have wider implications beyond who you include on the coffee run.

If you've been feeling negative about going to work, or
if your heart has sunk a little as you approach your office
or workplace, then it could be that the design of it simply
doesn't suit you. There are steps you can take to make your
workplace work for you.

Reworking our workspaces

A few years ago, I was introduced to the idea of a landscaped
workspace and I instantly saw the benefits as the best way to
design for cognitive wellness in the workplace. The idea of
cognitive wellness at work is to work in a way that supports your
brain's function. You can think clearly and problem-solve, you are
creative, you are focused and you can get into some deep work.
You also feel a positive sense of engagement and connection to
your work, and your mood is elevated by being in that space.

A landscaped workspace has different areas to meet different
needs, and offers flexibility to adapt workspaces to suit individual
needs. A landscaped workspace is easy to spot at first glance
because it does not have a uniform look and feel. As you glance
across the space, you will notice different levels and heights and
an array of different furniture. An engaging office space doesn't
need a slide or a ping-pong table but instead is designed with
different moods and needs in mind. Landscaped offices provide
that feel of gelling with your environment. It's an easy space
to connect with, because there is enough variety to suit you,
whatever you need. Everything about a landscaped office is
carefully considered to allow you to be at your cognitive best.

When you are designing an office for cognitive wellness there
are things to consider, and this goes for your own set-up at
home, as well as in the office. You need to be mindful of having
options, as many as you can, in a way that works for you. You
need the flexibility and adaptability to make your day work in

the way you need it to that day, and this can look very different throughout the week. We have differing levels of control over our workspace. Some of us will have the luxury of being able to design our surroundings, others will only have control over our individual desk or workspace. Whatever your level of influence over your workspace, there are ways of designing for cognitive wellness and it is well worth doing.

Start by stopping

Once again, we need to pause and reflect. The best workspaces are designed around different activities so grab a notepad and pen and start to write out all the different tasks and activities that you complete in your working day. Then think about what supports these activities. Do you need a clear desk? Space to spread out? A notepad to doodle or scribble on while you think? Do you need quiet, music, people or isolation? What works best to support you in these tasks?

We sometimes think that we don't have the time to pause and set up our workspace as we rush into our day, but this type of activity *gives* us time. Remember a decent workspace has the power to enhance creativity, boost happiness, build relationships, increase productivity and reduce stress. Taking the time to understand the way that we work best and then arranging our workstations around our needs gives us clarity, sparks creativity and joy, and allows us to focus – gaining us better results and higher engagement and satisfaction with our working day.

A natural workspace

A core principle of a great workspace is having a connection with nature, also known as biophilic design. Stephen Kellert, a professor of social ecology and one of the pioneers of biophilic design, describes this as 'the inherent human inclination to affiliate with nature that even in the modern world continues to be critical to people's physical and mental health and wellbeing'.[6]

Biophilic design seeks to connect us with nature as much as possible. We already know that nature can activate the parasympathetic nervous system, making us feel calmer and happier, and so it makes sense to bring as much nature into the workplace as we can. Nature can not only keep us happier in work, but keep us in work. Research shows that 10 per cent of employee absence can be attributed to workplaces with no connection to nature. In fact, the annual saving for a company by using biophilic design amounts to more than $3,000 per employee as absence is reduced and wellbeing is enhanced.[7] We also know that cognitive function and memory recall are improved by up to 25 per cent through biophilic design. That's a good reason to make your office space more in sync with nature. But how?

One of the best ways to connect with nature is to maximize natural light wherever possible. Exposure to natural light during the day supports our circadian rhythms, keeps us feeling alert and energetic, and helps to counter some of the negative impacts of blue-light exposure from our screens.

If you don't have ready access to a window, then consider investing in a daylight lamp, or swapping out your bulbs for daylight ones. Although not quite as good as the real thing, replicating natural daylight allows us to reap many of the same benefits as sitting near a window, and provides a better energy for us to work with.

Another way to connect with nature is to bring it indoors. Houseplants are a fantastic way to support biophilic design, and we can create interest and variety with different-shaped and -coloured leaves. Some offices really object to plants.

I have worked with companies that actually have written policies against plants in the workplace, which is literally unnatural and faintly ridiculous. The benefits of plants are wide and varied, and it is a simple and cheap quick fix to promote better health and happiness at work.

If you can't have access to real nature, then fake it. Hanging pictures of nature, using patterns and colour schemes that mimic nature, and adjusting lighting to imitate natural light fluctuations throughout the day offer the brain nature-like benefits.

Meet Eleanor

I work with nuclear materials and am in a bunker all day. Essentially, if something goes wrong, then the bunker is designed to collapse in on itself, thus minimizing radioactive materials escaping. It is a very necessary precaution for the work I do, but it makes for a depressing environment. I never see daylight or have any connection with nature. In the winter months I arrive at work in the dark, work in unnatural light, then leave in the dark. I was really sceptical about daylight bulbs and fake plants and pictures, but actually it really did help. I think because the work is safety-critical, the space had been really functional and we'd never paid attention to the look of the place, but you don't really want to climb into a dark and depressing bunker every day. Since we put daylight bulbs in, bright daylight welcomes me now, I feel as though I am climbing into sunlight. We have large pictures of forests to create a wall of trees and it is a really beautiful space. To be honest, I wasn't expecting it to make any difference to how I work, but I definitely enjoy my work more being in a beautiful space. I also became more aware of the importance of daylight and make a point of leaving the bunker on my lunch break and going for a walk, even if the weather isn't great, because it really re-energizes me. We reworked our workspace by bringing a connection to nature into the most unlikely environment. It has been a revelation and one we are continually looking to increase.

Taking time to create a workspace you want to be in is a great way to re-engage in both the space and the work itself. But what if you don't have control to redecorate or influence the wider office space? How do you create a great working environment just from your desk?

'Stage dressing' your workspace set-up

Setting your stage for work is key. We know our brains need physical cues to indicate that it is time to work. It is really important to have a designated and deliberate workspace. If you hot desk or work from home in a multifunctional space, such as at your dining table, stage dressing can tune you in. If you are trying to work in a space where you normally relax, then your brain needs to know that it is now time to focus and concentrate. This is why it is such a bad idea to try to work from your bed. Although it is tempting to stay comfy and snuggled and simply bring the laptop back to bed with you, the consequences of doing so can be hazardous for your sleep, your overall health and your relationships. Our brains are amazingly clever, but they rely on cues and pointers to make decisions.

HHSE boost: Reflection

Consider what you need to cue you into work. It's worth thinking about what helps you to work well and what distracts you. For example, if you struggle to take breaks, then you may want to keep a bottle of water and some snacks nearby to stop you becoming dehydrated or hungry. Whatever it is that is going to make you feel switched on to your tasks for the day, it's worth putting that in front of you.

Personally, I always need a notepad and pen next to me. I keep what I call my distraction list throughout the day, which is all the stuff that pops into my head when I am trying to work on something else. It could be anything from article ideas to a reminder to collect a prescription. Whatever it is, I scribble it down, getting it out of my head and allowing me to get on with my tasks. A notepad and pen are very portable and help me to focus, no matter what my workstation set-up is. The small ritual of laying them out works in a variety of places, whether I'm hot desking, in a coffee shop or at my kitchen table.

HHSE boost: Set your stage

Make a point of stage-setting your workspace every day for the next week. Follow the design principles of nature and natural light wherever you can, and set up your workspace with whatever you need to help you work better.

- How do you feel?
- What do you notice about your working week?
- What difference does the small routine of setting up for the day make to your motivation and engagement?

No matter where we work, if we can tune our brains in, then we find that we are automatically better able to concentrate, focus, stay motivated and have better stamina for enduring tasks.

Everything that has a place in our workspace needs a reason to be there and to serve a functional purpose. We don't need to be surrounded by distractions and clutter. Also a good set-up routine leads to a good wind-down routine, as we put these items away and signal to our brains that we are leaving our work zone and starting to tune into the rest of our lives.

Reworking our workspace

- Your workspace has the power to engage, motivate, uplift and energize you.

- It is challenging to find a workplace environment that suits everyone, so if you have struggled to connect with yours, then that's OK – there are small changes you can make to re-engage in your workspace.

- Even if you cannot control the wider environment, it is important to stage-set your workspace in ways that will work well for you.

- Bringing in nature, natural patterns and daylight wherever possible fulfils a deeper need to connect and makes us calmer, more productive and less stressed.

- Even if we constantly change and shift our workspaces, even a few small items can tune our brain in and help us re-engage with our work.

14

Reworking Work – Your Questions Answered

This book has delved into the many different aspects of how we work, and looked at where work needs reworking in order to better support and boost our health, happiness, safety and engagement. We have seen the positive impact of tuning into ourselves, reframing our mindsets, paying attention to our safety, being authentic and setting up a good workspace. We can also make sense of how many different aspects of work are not set up to best support us, and how we are being failed by the systems all around us, systems we have inherited from previous generations of workers and which we may ignore or walk past every day. We have seen the power of reworking our ideas, concepts, behaviours and environments and how these can radically improve how we feel about work. When we are safer and more engaged, we make healthier decisions and feel happier in ourselves.

In writing this book, I wanted you to see that if work hasn't been working out for you then it's not your fault. So much around us is unsupportive of the way that we work best, and it's important to recognize this, so that we stop blaming ourselves and become empowered to rework it. There is so much we can do, so much more power at our disposal, that is not role dependent. Our work isn't something that is done to us, leaving us to take the hit on our wellbeing regardless. We can rework our workplace, our teams and ourselves, no matter what role we are in.

When I started researching for this book, I asked people from all over the world, working in many different jobs and industries, the following question: 'What is the one thing you want to know about reworking work?'

I was inundated with questions, but there were some common themes that came up again and again, and so I have picked the most commonly asked to answer here. I hope these help you to rework some of the more painful parts of your working day.

How do I rework meetings?

Without doubt how to rework meetings was the most commonly asked question, and no wonder they cause problems. They are a regular feature in our work schedule, yet over half are considered a waste of time.[1] In fact, research conducted by the University of North Carolina found that 71 per cent of senior managers surveyed across various industries found meetings to be unproductive and inefficient. Moreover, 70 per cent of all meetings were found to keep employees from doing the work they were actually being paid to complete.[2] Instead of letting people do the job that they want and need to do, we keep them away from their work and locked in meetings (hopefully not literally!).

Of course, we don't just sit there wasting our time. Ninety-two per cent of us multitask during meetings, with 41 per cent of us multitasking in every meeting. So, we are working during meetings, and we're just not concentrating on the meeting we're in. Presenteeism at its finest, and not as productive as it sounds. The brain cannot really multitask, so if we are sitting in one meeting, but completing work for another, then we aren't really doing either well.

Meeting frequency seems to grow alongside seniority, with middle managers spending 35 per cent of their week in meetings. This increases to half the week once you reach senior management levels.[3] Working a five-day week, you are occupied by meetings the equivalent of Monday morning until mid-Wednesday before you actually get an opportunity to do some of your real work. This wouldn't be that bad if we could get all our meetings out of the way in one hit, gather up all the information we need and then progress with our work for the rest of the week. But meetings are peppered throughout our day, disrupting our thinking time and preventing progression.

We've probably all looked at the day ahead in our diary and planned what we want to achieve and then had our carefully thought-out day completely disrupted by last-moment requests for meetings ('Have you got time for a quick catch-up on XYZ …?'). Although a quick catch-up doesn't sound too problematic, 44 per cent of us find that sudden or unscheduled meetings mean that we don't have enough time to do our work.

An old habit of mine which I've never quite shaken is to work out the cost of each meeting and then ask myself, 'Is this meeting really worth the £XXX that it is costing?'

To this day I find it impossible to break this habit. You'd be amazed how often as a consultant I'm called into a meeting where people talk about efficiency and headcount reduction, with no recognition that this very meeting is costing the company hundreds of pounds which could be put to better use elsewhere.

How to rework meetings
Don't confuse availability with capacity

We, and others, confuse free space in our diary with the capacity to have a meeting. When we have a gap in our diaries, it can feel hard to defend that space. Technically it is free, so why are you declining that catch-up? The thing is, our work calendar is not just a list of slots to be filled with meetings. We need time to do our work, to complete tasks, to think. When we have back-to-back meetings, we often end up squeezing our work proper into the morning or evening on either side of our working day, whereas in fact we have paid hours when we should be completing it. Just because you can fit in a meeting does not mean that you should.

Go through and block out your diary. We get told this advice but often ignore it, not least because, when we go to block our diary, we discover that it's already full. Do something the future you will thank you for and block out future time in your diary, at a time that works for you, to get on with your work. This means that, when others check your diary looking for a meeting slot, they are more likely to work with times you won't object to.

If anyone comments on being unable to find a time in your diary, or having a lot of time blocked out, then be honest and say you're having to protect your diary to get your work done, and you don't have capacity for both. (I am yet to meet a manager who gets disgruntled when an employee is taking positive steps to get work done.)

Question your attendance

Don't automatically accept. We so often have meetings drop into our diaries and we automatically accept without reading the request properly, or asking whether or not we really need to be there. Question your attendance for every meeting and define what you will get out of it.

Reduce the time

Parkinson's law: if you give a meeting an hour, it'll take an hour. Go back and suggest 30 minutes for every hour-long meeting request you receive and see what the outcome is.

Share the load

If your entire team has to attend briefings or updates, then consider splitting the tasks among the team. Rather than everyone on the team attending, agree that one person will go and takes notes which they can share after the meeting. Then rotate that role, meaning only one person at a time on the team has to attend, freeing up the others' diaries. If you take notes during the meeting, then this is no extra work as you can type your notes directly into an email and hit send immediately afterwards.

Plan your cancelled meeting list

A last-minute cancellation can seem a real gift, especially in a very busy day. However, many of us lack the flexibility to be able to quickly adjust and effectively use that time well, and so end up wasting the gifted hour on emails, or inconsequential tasks, leaving us feeling that we've achieved nothing at the end of it.

One way around this is to create a list of small projects, ideas and research goals you want to do, and keep it handy. For example, it may be that you have an ongoing project which keeps falling to the bottom of the pile. Perhaps there are some people you need to reach out to, or a question you need to ask. By having a list nearby, you can quickly tick off a few tasks, which will feel ultimately satisfying and motivating, and also stop projects falling off the radar completely.

Say no with grace

Greg McKeown, author of *Essentialism: The Disciplined Pursuit of Less*, talks about saying no with grace, and it is a concept that is both fantastic and addictive. Once you start saying no with grace, you won't be able to stop. Saying no with grace means protecting your time and boundaries but not burning bridges. We sometimes don't say no because we fear being rude, but actually a clear no can be more graceful than a vague and unhelpful 'maybe' or 'I might be able to'.

I know you've asked for someone's help and been fobbed off with a 'leave it with me' only to chase them weeks later and receive a 'sorry I can't help you, I'm too busy'. Don't you find yourself thinking, 'Why didn't you just say no weeks ago and then I could have asked someone else?' Being vague is not being graceful. Delaying the eventual no often makes things much harder than just saying no outright, both on you and the person you are saying no to. No doesn't need to be rude, but it does need to be honest. If it's a no, then make it a no, not a maybe that you have no intention of following through with.

Let's say someone asks you to attend a regular weekly meeting. From the first meeting you join, you can see that this isn't a good use of your time as the team are still in the early planning

stages and they've invited you too soon. That's the perfect time
to decline with grace. Email or speak to the organizer and say
'I can see that this group is really important and I can definitely
help later down the line, but at this point I don't have anything
to add and I don't want to add to the participants unnecessarily.
Why don't you let me know when the team has specific
questions that I can help with and I'll come and join those
meetings, or email you my responses if I cannot attend?' This
is saying no gracefully. You are not making it all about you, and
you haven't said that this isn't important to you. But you have
got an hour back in your diary.

HHSE boost

Create a couple of stock responses for meeting
requests, so that you are ready to say no with grace. For
example, if you get asked to present a lot, you could
prepare a response that says, 'Thank you for thinking
of me – the conference sounds so interesting. Due to
tight diary constraints, I cannot commit to delivering
any presentations at this time. I'm sorry not to be
able to help on this occasion, but do consider me for
future events and I wish you every success with the
conference.' It's polite, it's a firm no, and it doesn't burn
a bridge. Perfect.

Use the technology

If you are being asked to share information again and again,
consider recording a presentation and adding the link to it to
an autoreply. This means your email will gracefully decline
on your behalf. An out of office message stating 'Thanks for

your email. If you are requesting a talk in relation to X, then unfortunately I don't have capacity to support individual team talks. However, you can find all the information and a recording to share *here*' can save you a lot of time and pressure.

This won't work for every ask, but it's worth considering who and what you can say no to, and then use the technology to your advantage.

How do I rework the team culture?

Trying to shift a whole team's attitude or culture can feel overwhelming and can leave us feeling stuck. We may not be able to change other people's behaviour but we can change our behaviour and interactions with other people. Remember the lily pad analogy – that when we move within our role, other people will move around us? The same is true of cultural changes. If we begin with our own behaviour, then the behaviour of those around us will change. This allows us to weave in more behaviour that increases our health, happiness, safety and engagement, and gradually changes a whole culture to be more HHSE focused.

I recommend the Japanese approach of kaizen. Kaizen is about small, daily, incremental improvements. Rather than setting huge goals, kaizen encourages small and gentle change which is designed to make a small improvement but which ultimately moves you towards your bigger goals.

I got asked to work with a team that was having a lot of difficulty and had become 'impossible to manage'. They were surly and disrespectful to leaders, they didn't turn up on time, and they were deliberately unhelpful around customer demands/deadlines. The manager felt completely overwhelmed and had no idea how to continue working with their team.

When I arrived on-site, the disrespect for the workplace was visible. The area around the building the team was based in was covered in cigarette butts and litter was blowing around all over the place. I knew what I was starting with.

I got introduced to the team and I asked for a site tour, starting outside. As we were walking around, I stopped to pick up the odd drinks can or crisp packet that was blowing around. The team leader noticed I'd stopped and said, 'Are you alright, Steph?' and I replied, 'Absolutely, just grabbing this – you all deserve better than to have litter blowing around you.' I didn't say anything else, and I didn't ask anyone else to pick anything up; I just kept walking.

Every day I worked with that team, I asked someone to walk me around the site and I picked up one or two pieces of litter and put them in the bin along the walk. I never asked for help or told people to clear the litter. However, the change started. Every day on my walk around the site, other people started picking up a piece or two of litter with me. One lunchtime, five members of the team announced they were going to 'sort out' the outside and grabbed litter pickers and brooms and swept the area clean. This was the first team activity they'd done in over a year. I hadn't suggested this; I had just quietly picked up one or two pieces of litter every day on my walk – a small, daily, incremental improvement. Kaizen. A new bin appeared, and a new cigarette butt disposal point was added. The manager began reporting a better sense of community within the team, and that there seemed to be a renewed respect for the workplace. Without any specific direction, the team changed how they were working together, and people were better organized. The team began to arrive at work on time, and they were more respectful of each other. They showed more interest in projects and customer deadlines. The manager introduced a large noticeboard where people could add their suggestions for improvements in the process, and they were given permission to try these out. Successful suggestions were implemented within the team and rewarded. The manager reported more respect, more engagement, more ease within the team.

If you need to change a whole culture, I recommend starting with a small, positive behavioural change that you yourself implement first. Where you lead, others will follow. It could be litter picking; it could be reframing an idea to offer a more balanced view; it could be thanking someone for their contribution. Whatever it is, start with your own behaviour and see what follows.

How do I rework my motivation?

We've talked about how the way we work at the moment leaves us in a constantly distracted state, and how the events of recent years may have left us feeling a little out of oomph. If motivation is lacking, then I recommend the following.

Start with your ikigai

What gets you out of bed in the morning? What lights you up? How can you bring more of that into your working day?

Reward yourself

We've discussed the importance of rewards, but remember they don't need to be big or expensive. It could be that every time you complete a task you reward yourself by listening to your favourite dance track or having a cup of your favourite tea.

Aim to put systems in place, not goals

James Clear, author of *Atomic Habits*, states: 'You do not rise
to the level of your goals. You fall to the level of your systems.'
Systems are the mechanisms that allow us to achieve our
goals. For example, if I have a goal to get fit, then I need a
system behind it – otherwise I will be initially motivated
and then, because I didn't create the system, I will forget to
exercise, get disheartened with my lack of progress, and lose
interest. The system we build around the goal 'get fit' might
be to take a walk every lunchtime. From here we can increase
our exercise, maybe swapping every other walk for a short
run. We will find it easier because the system of exercising
at lunchtime is already in place. By putting systems in place,
you are setting yourself up for continued progress, rather than
starting again every time.

Don't dismiss progress

Often, we aim for huge goals and dismiss smaller steps of
progress made along the way. Remember, our brains will sulk
and give up if we don't reward them, so instead focus on the
progress. Take the above example. If you want to get fit, then
you might think taking a walk every lunchtime won't be
enough, but it is certainly more progress than staying glued to
your chair. So ... reward yourself! Recognizing and rewarding
every step you make towards your greater goal will ensure
that you keep moving towards increased HHSE.

Divide (time) and conquer

I work in blocks of time and am a big fan of the pomodoro
technique where I work for 25 minutes concentrating solely

on one task without distraction, then take a five-minute break. I repeat this until the task is completed/I have hit that day's goal. However, if I am really struggling, then I set a timer for four minutes. I can't even really tell you why four; one day it just felt more doable than five, and I stuck with it! I'll then work on that project or task for just four minutes. It's not long, but it's long enough. Say I need to write a presentation but am struggling to get going. In four minutes, I can open PowerPoint, save a presentation file, choose the formatting and perhaps even write the opening slide or agenda for my presentation. It's not huge progress but it is some, and often, once I have got started, then I can keep going for much longer. Also, the task is less daunting by dint of the fact it's already started and some progress has been made, rather than see the day stretch ahead to complete a task, set a timer and work on that task for short bursts. Our attention is pulled in every direction throughout the day, so view these short bursts as gradually building up your concentration and motivation muscles. One day you can do four minutes and then you build up to eight and before you know it you can easily sit and concentrate for 30 and so on. See these bursts as a training programme to get concentration and motivation fit. You can do it!

How do I rework my terms – (aka how do I get a pay rise)?

It's fair to say quite a few people sent this question in as a jokey response, but as the saying goes, many a true word is spoken in jest, and digging a little deeper revealed an issue. Many people did want to know how to get more appreciation for the work they do, even if it wasn't financial, and these questions revealed a stronger urge to be recognized and valued.

One of the odd quirks of modern work seems to be that no news is good news. Unless we are in a role with inherent feedback – for example 'I am paid to process 20 reports per day and I either hit that target or don't' – then it can be genuinely hard to know whether or not we are doing a good job. We just don't hear back.

A survey conducted specifically looking at gratitude at work revealed that all participants recognized that saying thank you to colleagues makes them feel happier and more fulfilled, yet 60 per cent said they never express gratitude at work, or do so approximately once per year![4] We seem to be very ready to complain when something goes wrong, but rarely remember to praise when things go right, or when someone around us does a good job. You'll remember from the reworking your money mindset chapter that meaningful relationships at work cannot be built based on salary. People come to work for many reasons including respect and a sense of achievement and purpose. When we aren't appreciated, there are consequences and a direct hit to our HHSE score. Feeling underappreciated is a very real problem.

Research conducted on workers in the USA found that nearly half of those surveyed have left a job because they felt unappreciated, with 65 per cent of respondents saying they would work harder if they felt more appreciated. It seems the appreciation doesn't need to come from the top, with two-thirds of those surveyed saying they would stay working for an unappreciative boss, as long as their peers and co-workers showed recognition of their work. A simple 'thank you', 'great job' or the typically understated Brit comment 'nice one' can go a long way to making us feel seen and valued at work.

As for reworking your benefits, this can be a challenge, and the most effective starting point is to remove all emotion and, instead, gather evidence. It can be hard to disconnect emotion from money, particularly if we feel something is unfair or unjust, but conversations starting with 'It's not fair!' are unlikely to go anywhere productive. However, a solid evidence-based case will go a lot further. Here are my top tips for renegotiating your pay:

1 **Know your market value.** If you know what you are worth in the external market, then you can bring that as evidence to your conversation. Try to find roles similar to yours, in similar-sized companies, in order to demonstrate your market worth. If your role is a little unusual or niche, then try to find a breadth of positions with comparable responsibilities and accountabilities, in order to show what someone of your level and capability is earning even if it's not in your exact role. Many recruitment sites have a free salary checker which will tell you if your salary is above or below the market average. These are rough estimates, but it will give you a starting point.

2 **Be explicit.** If you want to discuss your salary, then be explicit in the meeting request. Ask your manager for a meeting to discuss your salary and benefits package. This can feel a bit scary, but catching them unawares can put the manager on the back foot and leave them feeling flustered, and this won't benefit you. I know many people who haven't got the conversation they wanted because their manager cancelled, was running late, or interrupted proceedings with another priority. If they know what you want to talk about and that it is important to you, then they can come prepared to listen and open to the

conversation. Being transparent makes it more comfortable for everyone.

3 **Don't make it a threat.** You can ask for a pay rise without having any intention of leaving, so be clear that you want to stay and this isn't a threat or an ultimatum (even if in your own mind it is!). It's useful to pin the request on a specific circumstance, such as following the successful completion of a project, the announcement of great financial results for the company, or after taking on additional responsibilities. Your annual performance review is also a good time to discuss your terms, as it is a natural point of reflection on your performance, and you will be setting objectives for the year ahead.

4 **Don't take no for an answer.** If you are greeted with a flat no, then clarify the next steps in the process. If your boss simply says no, then ask them when you can expect a review of your benefits and salary, what they would want to see you deliver or own before a renegotiation becomes possible, and in what timescale they see this happening. This prevents you being dismissed with a flat no and opens the door for future conversations.

5 **Don't take it personally.** If you are refused a raise or offered a lower sum than you have requested, it does not mean that your boss doesn't value you. In many large corporations there are fixed and inflexible payment grading structures which make it near impossible to progress someone's salary past a certain percentage. Gain clarity on the details and remain open to the conversation progressing at a later stage.

How do I rework my career?

A lot of questions on this theme seemed to relate to wanting to change role or career, or branch out and do something different but being uncertain whether it was the right thing to do.

Meet Kahlil

I've worked as a dentist for years, and most of the time I love my job, but over recent years I have had some health issues and in particular my gut health was bad. I sought all kinds of help, but medication and so on didn't really work for me, so I started to use food and changes to my diet to help and it fixed the problem. I got really interested in the impact of food on our health, physical and mental, and I think I'd love to do something in that field, but what do I do? I earn good money and I have a steady income. I'm a dad and need to provide for my kids. I can't just give up my job and go back to university, but the more time goes on, the more I think I could be doing something else. It's hard to let go of a career because what does a dentist know about anything other than teeth?! Where would I even start?

Kahlil, like many of us, didn't dislike his job, but he felt a pull towards something else that he thought could be interesting. He wanted to rework his job, but wasn't sure how and it was affecting engagement in his current work, as he was less interested in developing as a dentist when he thought he might be switching to something else.

Kahlil and I started by looking at his transferable skills and how he could use his current role to explore his interest. Kahlil had real doubts he could do something in nutrition yet had over ten years of patient experience in his role as a dentist. He was used to calming people, being kind and compassionate, and showing an interest in their health. In other words, he had many of the skills as well as the tact and compassion that would allow him to have conversations with people about their diet and gut health, and was far more equipped to switch to other career options than he first thought. It was his mindset that needed reworking, not his skillset.

Kahlil took many further steps, contacting health professionals specializing in his area of interest, and asking them to meet with him. He discussed with them their role, how they got into the work, and what pathways they would recommend for him. Kahlil also made contact with a university which was running a qualification aimed at working professionals and which he could thus complete at his own pace.

Kahlil gradually gathered all the information that he needed to allow him to take steps into a new career. He also sat down and did the maths on his salary and what a change in direction might look like. Essentially, Kahlil got everything he needed to make an informed decision.

If you want to change career and aren't sure where to start, then look at options or roles that appeal and that you see other people do, and investigate how they got there. Most people are very open to a chat about their work, and will take the time to help and advise you. Professional networks, such as LinkedIn, are a great starting point for this.

If you really don't know what you want to do, but you feel you want to do something else, then start with your values. What is it that matters most to you? What is it that lights you up? Then think about the opportunities that exist with interests and values like yours. Remember that we will have several different careers across our working lives, and so making a change doesn't mean you've made bad decisions in the past; it just means that you are ready for your next career move. Everything you've done, experienced and learned to date will support you with your next move, so don't worry if you are looking at other options. You're supposed to. You've reworked what you needed to and boosted your HHSE score. You are ready to work, well.

15

A Note on Quitting

I mentioned right at the beginning that I wasn't going to tell you to quit, at least not straight away. You needed to know and understand the four pillars of wellbeing and rework your working life before you could think about your next role. We know that if we want things to be different, but the only thing we change is our role, then our overall work life will stay the same.

Meet Di

I like to think of myself as a workaholic. I've always said that with real pride, but the truth is I like being needed and I like to think of myself as essential, like the whole place would fall apart without me. This hasn't served me well. Often, I've been taken advantage of because I say yes to everything, but then I resent it. I'll get overwhelmed and say to my boss, 'I can't cope with this, I'm leaving', and they'll tell me to push more onto my team and do less. But I really struggle. I left my last three jobs and wound up in exactly the same situation every time. What's worse is my last job was managerial and my approach just didn't work with the team. I would always leap in to solve everything. I thought they'd think I was a superhero, but my team feedback was that they felt micromanaged and as though I didn't trust them. They also said they were bored and weren't being stretched. I was constantly cursing my 'lazy' team, but did I actually give them anything to do? I swept in and tried to fix it all but … it wasn't useful, to them or me. I have had to do the work to rework my confidence and manage my sense of being needed, without relying on others to recognize me as a superhero. I still help people in my current role, but it's less about me and more about the team effort. It's been invaluable and I feel happier and more content than I have for ages.

Di is a great example of patterns repeating themselves. Unless we do the work to undo unhealthy work patterns, understand our triggers and unpick the myths, then we will remain stuck in unhealthy cycles which will affect us throughout our entire careers. This is why we shouldn't quit straight away, or as a knee-jerk response to a bad day. We first need to rework.

Once we've done the work and we understand what we want to do next, we may spot a really fantastic job and – hurrah! – we get the job offer and we accept! So now, we need to quit. How do we do it well, and how can we get one last boost for our HHSE score from our current role before we move on to horizons new?

Before you quit

1 **Do the rework.** Learn what it is that you need to make you happy, healthy, safe and engaged at work, and how you will take these ideas and skills into your next role.

2 **Know why you are leaving.** Is it that you want to leave the company? Is it that you've seen an amazing

opportunity elsewhere? Are you leaving for more money? Whatever your reason, knowing why you are leaving helps you make good decisions about what to do next and, potentially, what to avoid in your next role.

3 **Check the essentials.** How long is your notice period? Do you want to negotiate it? Is there a non-compete clause in your contract that could impact your next role? Being well informed protects you from any surprises once you quit.

4 **Ask yourself: 'Would anything make me stay?'** If your resignation prompts an offer of more money or a different position within your existing company, then being clear on why you are going and what, if anything, would make you stay is really useful. Don't be rushed to make a decision, as whatever they offer you may not change any of the fundamental reasons why you want to leave.

During your notice period

1 **Reflect on your current role.** Be clear in your own mind what you have learned from this role, and where you want to grow in your next role. Reframe any negative emotions. When you make the decision to quit a role, all kinds of emotion can be stirred up, ranging from relief, to anxiety, to a sense of failure. These are typical reactions to a big decision, and so we can reframe them as part of the process. Every job we have is a learning curve, and we all make mistakes throughout our working lives. In a survey of over a thousand employees, only 2 per cent reported no career regrets. We're allowed to learn, develop, make mistakes. Grant yourself enough psychological safety to

explore what worked, what didn't, what you tried and what you would do differently next time.

2 **Know that everything will suddenly look a lot better.** If you have been unhappy at work, or keen to leave for quite some time, then once you hand your notice in, work will suddenly be a lot more bearable. This is because you know you are leaving and so a lot of stress and pressure is lifted off your shoulders. This doesn't mean you have made the wrong decision in quitting; this is just one of the quirks of the process.

3 **Be realistic and don't own what isn't yours, including others' pressures and emotions.** People can act strangely once we've quit. Managers can set unrealistic expectations, so be really clear about how many days you have remaining in the company and what you can realistically achieve in that time. (One of my clients quit in March and was told by their manager that they needed to complete their entire year's objectives before they left ... They had a one-month notice period!) Needless to say, we reworked that expectation!

4 **Don't feel guilty.** People leave roles, and that's OK. People will have left before you and people will leave after you. It's not personal, so don't let anybody make you feel bad for doing what is right for you.

Once you've quit

1 **Take a break.** If you can, try to take a small break between roles. I know so many people who've left their old job on a Friday and started their new job the following Monday. This isn't a great idea as it doesn't allow you any

time to reflect and recover. The decision to leave is often a tough and emotionally laden one and the impact shouldn't be underestimated. A break to take care of your wellbeing can serve you well and ensure that you start your new role feeling energized and refreshed.

2 **Don't share more than you want to.** People often want the gossip, and it is so tempting to say something negative or share a frustration about a process in your old company. Don't. The only person this reflects badly on is you. If you were in a difficult position where you had to leave, then have a sentence or two prepared so you don't have to be pulled into a conversation that may upset you. If someone asks, 'Why did you leave your old company?', you can always reply, 'I was so excited about this role that I couldn't pass up the opportunity' or 'The advert for this really resonated with me and I knew there would be a great alignment with my values' or something similar. Obviously, once you form deeper and trusted relationships with colleagues you may be able to share more, but don't feel pressured into sharing what you don't want to.

3 **Let go of your old role.** Old colleagues may try to stay in touch and drop you a message about work-related issues. Remember, you don't work there anymore, and it is not your responsibility. Gently shut down those conversations. It's great to stay connected with friends at work, but if you are being used for your knowledge and information, then that's very different.

Most importantly, *remember your rework*. Keep close the knowledge of what works for you and how you reworked your work life to keep yourself happy, healthy, safe and engaged. Never settle for anything less.

Endnotes

Introduction

1 State of the Global Workforce (2022). *The voice of the world's employees*. Gallup Inc.

2 Dillard, A. (2013). *The writing life*. HarperCollins.

3 Statistic taken from the Gallup World Poll – which adds the proviso 'This estimate is conservative and may even be low; another estimate finds that people work over 115,000 hours in a lifetime' – State of the Global Workforce (2022). *The voice of the world's employees*. Gallup Inc.

1 Rethinking Work

1 Oswald, A. J., Proto, E., & Sgroi, D. (2015). Happiness and productivity. *Journal of Labour Economics*, *33*(4), 789–822.

2 OECD (2021). *Education at a glance 2021: OECD indicators*. OECD Publishing.

3 Dimovski, A. (2022). *20 eye-opening statistics about the state of career changes in 2022*. Go Remotely.

4 U.S. Bureau of Labor Statistics (2021). *Number of jobs, labor market experience, marital status, and health: results from a national longitudinal survey summary*. Economic News Release.

5 Meister, J. (2012). *The future of work: job hopping is the 'new normal' for millennials*. Forbes.

6 Brookes, A. C. (2021). *A profession is not a personality*, How to Build a Life Series. The Atlantic.

7 Steel, D. (2022). *Parental guidance: careers information and advice*. Careers Writers Association.

8 Wood, J. (2018). *104 countries have laws that prevent women from working in some jobs*, Workforce and Employment: World Economic Forum.

9 Nielsen, J., Zielinski, B., Ferguson, M., Lainhart, J., & Anderson, J. S. (2013). An evaluation of the left-brain vs right-brain hypothesis with resting state functional connectivity magnetic resonance imaging. *PLoS ONE*, *8*(8), e71275.

10 Clear, J. (2018). *Atomic habits: an easy and proven way to build good habits and break bad ones*. Penguin Random House.

11 Gaetano, C. (2015). Study: people overestimate how long they work by about 5–10 percent. *The Trusted Professional*, NYSSCPA.

12 Branson, R. (2016). *My metric for success? Happiness*. LinkedIn, available at linkedin.com/pulse/my-metric-success-happiness-richard-branson?trk=mp-reader-card

2 Start by Stopping

1 Danziger, S., Levav, J., & Avnaim-Pesso, L. (2011). Extraneous factors in judicial decisions. *Proceedings of the National Academy of Sciences*, *108*(17), 6889–92.

2 Carr, C. (2014). Doctors more likely to prescribe antibiotics later in the day. *The Pharmaceutical Journal*, 8 October, available at pharmaceutical-journal.com/article/news/doctors-more-likely-to-prescribe-antibiotics-later-in-the-day#fn_1 (last accessed 16 November 2022).

3 Beyond Money to the True Value of Work

1 Many versions of this story are in circulation, but the original story seems to have been told by the German author Heinrich Böll.

2 Cameron, J., Banko, K. M., & Pierce, W. D. (2001). Pervasive negative effects of rewards on intrinsic motivation: the myth continues. *The Behaviour Analyst*, 24(1), 1–44.

3 Kohn, A. (1993). Why incentive plans cannot work. *Harvard Business Review*, September–October, available online at hbr.org/1993/09/why-incentive-plans-cannot-work

4 Sandberg, S. (2015). *Lean in: women, work, and the will to lead*. WH Allen.

5 Bajorek, Z. (2018). *Employee Assistance Programmes (EAPs) supporting good work for UK employees?* Work Foundation.

6 Knight, R. (2017). How freelancers can make sure they get paid on time. *Harvard Business Review*, 15 August, available at https://hbr.org/2017/08/how-freelancers-can-make-sure-they-get-paid-on-time (last accessed 16 November 2022).

4 Do No Harm

1 Katwala, A. (2016). *The athletic brain: how neuroscience is revolutionising sport and can help you perform better*. Simon & Schuster.

2 Chandola, T. (2010). *Stress at work: a report prepared for the British Academy*. British Academy Policy Centre.

3 Stone, L. (2012). The connected life: from email apnea to conscious computing. *HuffPost*, 7 May, available at huffpost.com/entry/email-apnea-screen-apnea_b_1476554 (last accessed 16 November 2022).

4 Hackeling, E. (2020). How much time are you spending on email? *front.com*, 17 April, available at front.com/blog/how-much-time-are-you-spending-on-email

5 Scott, E. (2020). Using shopping as a stress reliever. *Verywellmind.com*, 22 November, available at verywellmind.com/retail-therapy-and-stress-3145259 (last accessed 16 November 2022).

5 Psychological Safety

1 Vargas, S. (2021). *Psychological safety: a hot concept in management, can it help create safer workforces?* Safety & Health, A National Safety Council Publication.

2 Giles, K. (2018). Why you mistakenly hire people just like you. *Forbes*, 1 May, available at forbes.com/sites/forbescoachescouncil/2018/05/01/why-you-mistakenly-hire-people-just-like-you/ (last accessed 16 November 2022).

3 Clark, T. (2020). *The 4 stages of psychological safety: defining the path to inclusion and innovation.* Berrett-Koehler.

4 De Smet, A., et al. (2021). *Psychological safety and the critical role of leadership development.* People & Organizational Performance, McKinsey & Company.

5 Edmondson, A. (2014). Building a psychologically safe workplace. TEDx talk, available at youtube.com/watch?v=LhoLuui9gX8 (last accessed 16 November 2022).

6 Leary, M. R., & Kowalski, R. M. (1990). Impression management: a literature review and two-component model. *Psychological Bulletin, 107*(1), 34–47.

7 Redford, G. (2019). Amy Edmundson: psychological safety is critically important in medicine. Association of American Medical Colleges (AAMC).

8 Petzer, M. (2020). Don't shoot the messenger: the enigmatic impact of conveying bad news during redundancy situations and how to limit the impact. The shifting landscape of work and working lives, CIPD Applied Research Conference 2020.

9 Fitzgerald, S. (2022). Employees don't have survey fatigue – they are tired of being ignored. *Insight*, 16 March, available at workplaceinsight.net/employees-dont-have-survey-fatigue-they-are-tired-of-being-ignored/ (last accessed 16 November 2022).

7 Are You Stressed Yet?

1 Division of Population Health (2018). *Mental health in the workplace*. National Center for Chronic Disease Prevention and Health Promotion.

2 Fisher, J. (2015). Workplace burnout survey: burnout without borders, *Deloitte*, deloitte.com/us/en/pages/about-deloitte/articles/burnout-survey.html (last accessed 16 November 2022).

3 Marling Company and the American Institute of Stress (2009). *The Workplace Stress Scale: attitudes in the American workplace VII*.

4 Wardele, S. (2019). Ten-minute appointments too short to be useful and must be phased out by 2030, say GPs. *Independent*, 21 May, available at independent.co.uk/news/health/gp-appointments-ten-minutes-phase-out-2030-royal-college-nhs-a8922106.html (last accessed 16 November 2022).

5 Suff, R. (2022). Stress in the workplace: learn how to identify the signs of stress, address stress at work, and distinguish between stress and pressure. CIPD (Factsheets).

6 Digital Information World (2018). Social media use during work hours by employees (infographic), digitalinformationworld.com/2018/09/problems-social-media-workplace.html (last accessed 16 November 2022).

7 Haynes, T. (2018). Dopamine, smartphones & you: a battle for your time. *Science in the News*, 1 May, Harvard University, available at sitn.hms.harvard.edu/flash/2018/dopamine-smartphones-battle-time/

8 Haynes, T. (2018). Dopamine, smartphones & you: a battle for your time. *Science in the News*, 1 May, Harvard University, available at sitn.hms.harvard.edu/flash/2018/dopamine-smartphones-battle-time/

8 Burnout

1 ICD-11 for Mortality and Morbidity Statistics (version 02/2022).

2 Fogarty., P., et al. (2020). Coronavirus: how the world of work may change forever. BBC: Work Life Series, available at bbc.com/worklife/article/20201023-coronavirus-how-will-the-pandemic-change-the-way-we-work (last accessed 16 November 2022).

3 Richter, F. (2022). The Great Resignation record: how many Americans left their jobs in November 2021? Workforce and Employment, World Economic Forum.

4 Tanzi, A. (2022). Millions regret quitting their jobs during the Great Resignation. *Financial Post*, 12 July, available at https://financialpost.com/fp-work/millions-regret-quitting-great-resignation

5 Organisation for Economic Co-operation and Development (2020). *Work-life balance.* Better Life Index.

6 World Health Organization (2021). Long working hours increasing deaths from heart disease and stroke. WHO and ILO.

7 Pratt, L. (2018). 97% of office workers feel frustrated at work. *HRD Connect*, 21 November, available at hrdconnect.com/2018/11/21/97-of-office-workers-feel-frustrated-at-work/ (last accessed 16 November 2022).

9 Being Your Authentic Self at Work

1 Johnson, A. (2021). One in five adults 'cannot be their true self at work' – research. *Yorkshire Live*, 24 November, available at examinerlive.co.uk/news/uk-world-news/one-five-adults-cannot-true-22256729 (last accessed 16 November 2022).

2 Bigelow, L. (2022). Adult behaviour patterns in the workplace. *Chron*, available at smallbusiness.chron.com/adult-behavior-patterns-workplace-12249.html (last accessed 16 November 2022).

3 Mary Portas quoted in [tbc].

11 Reworking Teamwork

1 Murphy, Jr, B. (2019). Gallup calls this 8-word question its 'most controversial' ever. (But a new survey of 2000 workers shows it's what employees care about most). *Inc.*, inc.com/bill-murphy-jr/gallup-calls-this-8-word-question-its-most-controversial-ever-but-a-new-survey-of-2000-workers-shows-its-what-employees-care-about-most.html (last accessed 16 November 2022).

2 Tuckman, B. (1965). Developmental sequence in small groups. *Psychological Bulletin, 63*(6), 384–99.

12 Working Alone

1 Morton, B. (2022). Workers going into the office 1.5 days a week, survey suggests. *BBC News*, available at bbc.co.uk/news/business-62542537 (last accessed 16 November 2022).

2 Study conducted by Voucher Cloud surveying nearly 2,000 UK workers. Available at vouchercloud.com/resources/office-worker-productivity (last accessed 16 November 2022).

3 Zhang, S., Liu, P., & Feng, T. (2019). To do it now or later: the cognitive mechanisms and neural substrates underlying procrastination. *WIREs Cognitive Science, 10*(4).

4 Bisin, A., & Hyndman, K. (2018). *Present bias, procrastination and deadlines in a field experiment.* National Bureau of Economic Research.

13 Reworking Our Workspace

1 Sander, E. (2021). Science confirms it: open offices are a nightmare. *Fast Company*, available at fastcompany.

com/90652947/science-confirms-it-open-offices-are-a-nightmare

2 Sander, J. E., et al. (2021). Open-plan office noise is stressful: multimodal stress detection in a simulated work environment. *Journal of Management and Organization*, 27(6), online.

3 Work in Mind (2020). Does poor workplace design lead to more sick days? New research suggests yes, available at workinmind.org/2019/09/16/does-poor-workplace-design-lead-to-more-sick-days/

4 Business First Your Space to Work (2016). Hot-desking is revolutionising modern business, but is it worth it? Available at businessfirst.co.uk/news/hot-desking-is-revolutionising-modern-business-but-is-it-worth-it/#:~:text=Does%20hot-desking%20work%3F%20 Well%2C%20there%20is%20a%20strong,space-saving%20 technique%20of%20hot-desking%20in%20their%20 office%20spaces (last accessed 16 November 2022).

5 López, N. H. (2022). Neurodiverse design: how to create inclusive workspaces. *Exceptional Individuals*, available at exceptionalindividuals.com/about-us/blog/neurodiverse-design-how-to-create-inclusive-workspaces/

6 Cited by TSK (2021). *Biophilic design – naturally great.* TSK Wellbeing.

7 Gloede, K. (2015). 7 ways to enhance indoor environments with biophilic design. *The Journal of American Institute of Architects*, 17 February, available at architectmagazine.com/technology/7-ways-to-enhance-indoor-environments-with-biophilic-design_o (last accessed 16 November 2022).

14 Reworking Work – Your Questions Answered

1 Chang, C. (2020). Shocking meeting statistics in 2021 that will take you by surprise. Productivity Hacks Blog, Otter.

2 Gourani, S. (2021). Why most meetings fail before they even begin. Leadership Strategy, *Forbes*, available at forbes.com/sites/soulaimagourani/2021/05/06/why-most-meetings-fail-before-they-even-begin/ (last accessed 16 November 2022).

3 Borsellino, R., et al. (2020). How much time do we spend in meetings? (Hint: It's scary). *The Muse*, available at themuse.com/advice/how-much-time-do-we-spend-in-meetings-hint-its-scary (last accessed 16 November 2022).

4 Kaplan, J. (2012). *Gratitude survey. Conducted for the John Templeton Foundation*. The Berkeley University Press.

Acknowledgements

A huge thank you to Jonathan Shipley at Nicholas Brealey for his time, energy and encouragement in bringing this book to life. Also thank you to Victoria Roddam for her continuing faith and confidence in my writing, and for being the giver of gentle nudges when needed!

Thank you to everyone who has reworked their working lives with me. It is such an honour to see you blossom and grow within your careers, at all ages and stages, and I am thrilled to see you thrive. I am proud of each and every one of you.

Last, and most definitely not least, thank you to Matt. Endless hours listening to me, alongside many miles walked with the dogs so that I could write without their 'help', are so, so, so appreciated. You are a total star, and I love you.